T0165320

Journey to Self:
Journey to Love

Raechel "Dr. Rae" Rivers

authorHOUSE®

AuthorHouse™
1663 Liberty Drive
Bloomington, IN 47403
www.authorhouse.com
Phone: 1-800-839-8640

First published by AuthorHouse 7/1/2011

ISBN: 978-1-4634-0709-4 (sc)
ISBN: 978-1-4634-0710-0 (e)

Printed in the United States of America

Any people depicted in stock imagery provided by Thinkstock are models,
and such images are being used for illustrative purposes only.
Certain stock imagery © Thinkstock.

This book is printed on acid-free paper.

Raechel Rivers
I Believe
January 23, 2008
(Class Assignment)

The Right Time

Lately, something that has been getting to me is the fact that I am 27 and single. Now in my mind I know that there is not a thing wrong with that simple fact. When I look around at my outer world, I see relationships, relationships, everywhere!! So I wonder, will I ever have the chance to experience one of these, what appears to be, intimate relationships? The kind of relationship that I'm speaking of is that of man/woman or husband/wife. I know that as a single person I do not know what it means to be married; only a married person could tell me. Different people that I've talked to give me different information about being married, some of it is good and some not so good. I guess in a world of "yes I am single and dating until I meet the right person", I am okay with focusing on other things right now. I am trying to get into the habit of practicing this instead of worrying so much about being single. I have a few dates here and there, but I still haven't met someone who suits me, or it could just be bad timing. I believe that timing is everything. How does that sound coming from a young woman who has developed a reputation for being habitually late? I believe that situations, circumstances, and people change everyday. I believe that I am definitely a product of my environment. I also believe there is a "special force" keeping me moving in a positive direction in my life. I would not be where I am today without a divine essence allowing "good" things to happen in my life. Even when I don't always make the right decisions, it seems that things just turn out right. A series of failed relationships has taught me that when I am unfocused on myself and my aspirations, things tend to fall apart. If I can't keep myself together, organized, and prepared, how will I be able to provide for a husband and children. With all of this said, I still hope that there is someone special out there for me, and I believe it can only happen if and when the time is right.

This is dedicated to a Divine Soul I once met...my encounter with You allowed me to experience a new level of Love which in turn brought me back to my True Self. "We have many Soulmates but only one Twin Flame" (Alexyss K. Tylor, 2009). If you are not my Twin, you surely lit my Fire; and taught me to fall in Love with what I do. No one can take what we love away from us. It is our True Essence and our Assignment from God. I send you Peace, Prosperity, and Love all the days of your life Darryl.

This is also dedicated to my Mother, Karen D. McFerren Rivers Martin, who was my first Teacher. Without her dedication to education, I would not have been the intellectually advanced child God created; but she nurtured. Your love and encouragement has sustained me for thirty years. I thank God for you.

This book is also for women and young women everywhere. The most important aspect of the journey to self and the journey to love is learning. Learn who you are; and learn from the bumps in the road. You will reach your destination.

To my Dad, William "Ray" Rivers, keep resting in peace; and thank you for watching over me and protecting me along with an army of other Angels.

To my Dad, Lance A. Martin, thank you for being such a great friend and supporter of all my "grand" ideas; and we know the sky is the limit. You taught me "the decisions we make are for life".

To my Biggest Fans; my Big Brother Rapheal, my Sister Carmenita, my Granny Dorothy McFerren, my Auntie Shirley, my Godparents the Mozees, my Godmother Lynne Henderson, and my Auntie Renee'...thank you for always praying and supporting me in all that I choose to pursue!

To my Life Mentor, Michelle Lang Smith, my "Soul Sistah" Tena, my "Twin" Crystal, my Cousin Liz, my Bestie Nikia, my Prayer Warrior Faaizah, my O.G. Raegan, First Cousin Javeline; and my other girls Cousin Martina, Lynesia, Karie, Carolyn, and Molly, thank you for being great listeners; for your critiques of my work; and for relationships that come without judgment...you are my Sisters!

To my Niece Chelsy, this is for you too! When you reach my age, you will then fully understand why you had so many haters. They hate cha 'cause they ain't cha! God has blessed you with so many gifts and talents...You are beautiful, and don't let anyone tell you otherwise! I love you!

There are so many others, family and friends, who have supported me along this journey. You are appreciated. Thank You!

Table of Contents

Part II
Reality Check: Wake Up!

Part III
A Work in Progress: Learning

Part IV
Self-Love: Walk the Talk

Part V
Rebirth: The Journey Continues

Extras!

Introduction:
Why the Journey to Self?

We all have a journey or a path that has been laid before us since we entered this world. It is a God mandated journey, or else why would we be here? We didn't create ourselves; so it is our duty to find out or remember why we were created. What were we born to do? How can we contribute to the world we live in to make it a better place where all can live in peace and harmony? This is a lofty ideal, but the truth is one day we will make our way back to our Creator; God, the Source of Love, Abundance, Peace, Prosperity, Joy, Wellness, and Life. I believe that it will be asked of us, "Did you do your part?" "Did you complete your assignment?" We may have many assignments or we may be assigned to many people, but ultimately, we must learn how to do what we were born to do.

During my short 30 years of life, I've experienced so much about "love" and relationships. I trust that we all have experienced our fair share. What if your experiences and being healed from the lessons learned are a part of your assignment from God? Now who signs up for heartache and pain? Not one of us. If these experiences can be used to help a younger generation or to help heal another, I'm ready to share. What I've learned about love is that it is a journey just like life! Sure it hasn't all been roses and it hasn't all been heartache, but it has been a road that has led me back to my first love; God, my Creator. This is the refreshing part of the journey. This is the part of the journey where all of Heaven and the Angels rejoice in knowing that we have remembered the One who first loved us. There is no greater love. So I say that, *"love is a journey where you go searching and ultimately find yourself"*. You find the God that is within and the God who created you. You remember what you were born to do!

The Journey to Self

The world at age 29 looks a whole lot different than it did twenty years ago. Well, at least that's expected. Now let's look back about ten years. Yes, the world and my perspective of it is changing daily. Is it true what they say? The more things change, the more they stay the same. Whoever came up with that one? I can see the truth in that one. When I think about my hometown, family, and old friends, then the old saying holds true. No matter what you go through in life, inner and outer changes, career changes, relationship changes; there is something about home that should give you a sense of security and balance. Family and home give you somewhere to return to, even if it's temporary, when life begins to feel out of your control. Some may not have this type of safe-haven to escape to from their lives, but there is no greater feeling than being able to have a place to go or people to call on when the burdens of life overwhelm you. I have to agree; there really is" no place like home".

"Home" for some may not be home for others. As we observe some of the tragic events taking place in our nation at this time, and the destruction of communities whether by homicides or natural causes, we see that some of us have no home of which to return. So as we mature, we realize that there is so much work to be done within and without to even maintain that sense of balance afforded us by home and family. We learn to nurture ourselves despite our circumstances instead of reaching for an external haven of peace, which is usually temporary anyway. We discover that the "burdens" of life are only temporary as well. If we can master achieving peace within, then our external conditions are unable to disturb us. The art of mastering peace within takes some work. As children, all we had to do was just cry about it and Mom or Dad or Grandma and Grandpa would fix it. However, becoming an adult truly requires developing and maintaining our own self-sufficiency. Not in a sense that we don't need others, but we have to know that there's a resolve to situations, even if it's not an instantaneous one. Now try to explain that to the microwave/technology savvy generation we've grown up in and are further creating. We want instant results!

We can see the example of wanting instant results in the way we operate in our relationships and even in the workplace. Instant gratification can actually become an addiction. Technology has truly evolved the entire way we see, do, and communicate in our world today. We generally want "a lot for a little". We want all the glory of a new job or relationship, but don't want to start at the bottom and work our way up or into something great. Hey, we are very needy people from the money department to the love department. Some of us may be in denial about "needing" love, but we all need it. Yes, we have the love from within, but let's just face it, again there is nothing like having the external love from family, children, friends, and/or a significant other. Again, when we become out of balance even in the love department, it may cause us to act in desperation mode. This is unhealthy and only winds up keeping us from the love we truly desire. So we must return to the home or the love within in order to truly become balanced; these are the signs of maturity.

The end of our twenties and crossing over into the thirties, sometimes make us feel a sense of desperation toward our life goals, if we aren't doing what we want, and our relationship goals. We start to think, "I'm so old now", or "I was supposed to be married by now". Also, how about, "my life is over!" These are very comical statements huh? This type of thinking is the furthest thing from the truth. We have to know and trust that everything is in Divine Order in our lives, and that the state of our current life and or relationship situations is due to whatever we did yesterday. For every action, there is a reaction. As for yesterday, now is the time to let go. Now is the time to begin building toward our goals, especially if our circumstances are displeasing to us. We will no longer live in "shoulda, coulda, woulda". Whether you are 30, 40, or even 50 plus, it's never too late to do what your heart desires. You can have the "good life" that you desire. Sure, some work is in order, but undoing the mistakes from our pasts, if they were unhealthy, takes time. I don't know how long it's going to take, but I do know that giving up is not an option for me.

We have to develop a clear picture of what we want and know that the Universe will deliver. We have to find out or re-visit our special gifts and talents; the thing that we are best at or that we know God has placed within us. We need to realize who we are, and find out how we can contribute to our dream and help others along the way. Living this life is not just about us. That is not why God created us. In fact that is a selfish way to live, and we know of people who live this way. The world revolves around them. Maybe we've even been that person a time or two, but again that's the difference between thinking as a child and thinking as a mature adult. We all must play our part.

One Day at a Time

What's the rush? Your life in this lifetime won't end until God says so; that is if you are living happy and healthy. Sometimes our lifestyle or choices can lead us to an early grave. So we must learn how to live, even if it takes re-programming our beliefs about life, which could in turn lead us to live a longer life. The truth is our habits, thoughts, actions, and character create the life we choose to live. If we choose to fill our days with healthy eating and thinking, then long days are ahead of us. Once we realize the path toward wellness, we can begin to truly live! We begin to understand what God wants us to do in the time that is allowed. There is a huge dying world out here. What can we do to live well or get our "piece of the pie" as well as help others? Those who live unselfishly will always have a reserve stored up of people who can help them when they need it. It is not always the people you bless who bless you, but your blessing can come from others. Sometimes even strangers! The Golden Rule still remains; "do unto others", and there are Karmic Laws that exist. Remember, "What goes around comes around". So don't be upset when someone has wronged you and don't seek revenge or to wrong others. Keep living your life for the blessings that are in store for you.

Cultivating this peace within or "Christ" consciousness takes maturity and takes some work. Some of us are just born this way. The world laughs at us because of the fact that people seem to always get over on us and not vice versa. Believe me; the people getting over will have a price to pay some way or another. Don't dwell on how someone has wronged you. Just take life one day at a time and be thankful for the lesson you learned in dealing with that person or situation. Slow down and appreciate all the good things in your life. Your life is not going anywhere and besides you have so much work to do on what God wants you to do. You have time to do these things and to live, but you don't have time to worry about your past. Healing from the past can take some time and once you have freed yourself from hurt and pain, you can get to work. Use your time wisely!

Wow! Three decades of life! I still can't believe this! What will 30 be like? This is a celebration of life! This is a time to reflect on what's next for my life. What do I truly desire? What have I learned along the way? How can I begin to live for true happiness, wellness, and walk in abundance? These are just some of the questions that come to my mind. I'm ready to embark upon this new path; this part of the journey. They say life begins at 30. I believe this is true. This is a time of maturity. This is a time when people start to realize that "it's not about me"; that God wants me to do something. Some people find this maturity long before thirty, but for others, I'd say three decades of life is a definite turning point. This is a time of liberation and to embrace who you are. By this time, you truly begin to know thyself. You've experienced the growing pains of the teen years and the ones of the twenties, and the light bulb just seems to illuminate! As you can see, I'm excited about what the thirties have in store. I feel that everything I've learned until now can be used to help me create the "good" life that I desire. We all must define our own happiness and good life. One may be content or have the desire to live a simple life, while others may want to "gain the whole world". Not for the price of your soul though.

Thirty is also a time when some people start really settling down speaking in terms of relationship and career wise. We finally start to figure out what we want to do and do it well. I'm excited about the settling down part. Well, of course, I'm the "Love Doctor"! People who "find" their Soul Mates at this time or even before 30 have truly mastered some things. They know what God wants them to do, and they have also matured from the "it's all about me" phase. If we are not whole within ourselves and we wander around aimlessly still trying to figure out what to do, it will be difficult for a Mate to be added to our life. In a way, we repel this person by not being healed and by not knowing what we want from life. Also, we have to realize that a Mate is not for us. He or she is for God. God blesses the union for a purpose. There is something that God wants the two to do together. This is why the two become one. If I don't know what God wants me to do, how can I be successful in a union? I don't think this is a situation that will last very long because eventually the give will outweigh the take. It's funny because we've all heard people say that your Mate comes along when you're not looking. So true; I believe because at the time you are so focused on what God wants you to do, and so is your Mate. The two of you will be able to find each other in a situation that will require you to do something together as well as complement each other. I believe that few of us find this in the times we are living in, but this may be because of so many imbalances in our earth and society at this time. All I can say is keep believing and do what God wants you to do. This person may be right under your nose, but keep working on you and fostering your life and your interests. This is the way to truly attract a balanced Mate. He or she will be a reflection of you. The "journey to self" is the journey to love; true love, God and your Mate. Don't find yourself just settling down with someone just for the sake of settling down. You will miss the entire purpose of God and the union. You must truly know yourself and be patient.

Take Control of Your Life

Sometimes taking control of your life is as easy as letting go! Sound complicated? The truth is that the more we hold on to things that aren't in our control, events, people, etc., the worse we make the situation. We have to know that there's a Higher Power acting in our favor. If you believe, you will receive. The things that need controlling are our actions and reactions to situations. Do what you can, and God will do the rest. The Universe will always provide what you ask of it. We create our experiences and our life by the activities we engage in daily. What we do today, truly affects our tomorrow. So why not engage in activities that will assist us in having the life that we desire; the healthy body and mind we desire; and the love-relationships we desire. Taking control of what you can control is never easy or a quick fix. Old habits die hard. Your body will crave the substances that you are trying to rid from it. Your mind will want to resort to negative thinking when you have a bad day. In order to change, you must truly desire the changes, and do something small daily toward your goal or end result. The choice is yours to take control and let go; let God!

Part I

The Ideal of Love: Joy & Pain

In Love with Love
(2010)

I am in love with love...
I don't want to be...
I do but I'm so afraid...
Maybe this time, it will work
Are you here...
Should I write about you like the others?
Why are you here?
Am I forcing you to be?
Us to be...
Are you that reflection of me?
I am in love with you...
The idea of you...
The idea of us...
Could it really be?
I feel like giving up on love
Naturally...
I want you...
Make this go away
If it's not true
I'm not this open
I want you in every way
Not just physically
But mentally, spiritually and emotionally
How do we get there?

I think we're almost there
Work with me...
Flow with me
I feel you
Connecting with me
Are you scared of this love thing?
Let's see how far we can go...
Love, love, love
I am in love with love...

*W*hy do some women like myself find ourselves asking questions such as:
1. Why am I still single?
2. When is my "Prince" going to come along?

Let's take a deeper look inside: I can only speak from my own experiences and not for the whole species of women...I tend to take the blame for most of my relationships gone wrong...I try not to blame the men...although, I do have many complaints.

So where does the Mis-Education come into play... living in a fantasy in your head...or from watching too many romance movies on TV. Yes, wait on God, even when you are up to no good. I believe that God never stops working...there is a lesson in every relationship gone bad. Not being patient enough with yourself or with men...being too anxious. Is this a such thing? Desiring the "good" thing (relationship) is a natural desire. But it should not be the complete focus.

So now what? Currently, I am trying to change my approach to the dating scene. I am beginning to weed out the ones who only want to be around for some you know what...yes, this can be difficult, but how long does it take to realize that the road is going nowhere?

So when is it right to give into sex in a relationship? I can't answer that...but make sure you will be respected in the morning. How do you go from a physical relationship to one that has a foundation? Some say that you don't.

I think that a lot of it has to do with the "Self". When we are right within ourselves and looking for nothing and lacking nothing...then we will attract the right person...again...I am more so venting than giving advice...I'm a work in progress.

I don't have the definitive answers...but I'm going to keep on waiting and searching...until I find and am found...ya know? Meanwhile...I am working on me the best way that I can and getting rid of the "fakers" somebody who is full of crap and not wanting me for me...if you have to change too much...it ain't worth it! Know yourself first...so that a good man will recognize the real you. Trust God...not Man...that "good" thing is out there. He does exist; because hey...you exist.

Wooing my infatuation...thinking of a Master Plan to make you mine...

Not by force or desperation...just smart enough to know it may take some time

Patience...just let me love you

Loving you is what keeps me alive

Without love I'm just existing...

But with love...I'm beautiful, powerful, vibrant, motivated...

I'm here for the long-run...til time runs out of time

Or our season together comes to an end...

My Everything...my friend...

Whatever you need...please don't look any further...

It's me...as long as you let me be...

If you can receive...I'm here to give...

So wide open...

I don't want to be...

But I'm so caught up...

It supersedes the physical realm

What I feel comes from a place so spiritually unreal...

That my words cannot explain...

I know it's not in vain,

I know it's meant to be for this moment in time...

I had to experience this thing...

You...

Divine Appointments

*J*believe in "Divine Appointments". My Life Mentor first introduced me to this concept. Divine appointments can occur in relationships with family and friends, love relationships as well as people you don't know (those you meet in passing or those you meet for the first time)... have some of us unknowingly entertained Angels? Divine appointments are unplanned events/meetings with people... Regarding love relationships; this can be a joyous time! It's like really liking someone, wanting to see them or talk to them and they walk by or call! It's like praying and searching for your Soulmate, and meeting him or her the next day. God and our Angels set these things in motion...whether this person is here for a Season or a Lifetime, they come into your life for a purpose...it is something that you can feel in your soul. You know what you need, and they are there to provide it...it could be in conversation; exchange of ideas; healing; networking...you name it...you learn something in all these divine appointments.

I have been encountering several of these lately...with many people...not just love interests. I have also been getting in tune with my Angels. Google Doreen Virtue and you will know what I'm talking about. Our angels will help us bring desires to pass. Regarding love, I've often gone in with "rose-colored" glasses on...hmm...doesn't that feel like the best of times? It is important to maintain communication with your love interest so that you will know if you are both on the same page. Lack of communication is one of the things that make dating and relationships so difficult. What happens when you take off your tinted shades? When all the truth is revealed? Will you be able to love unconditionally? Will you be able to let someone go if their season in your life has ended? We must pray everyday and hope for the best in our dating life, and constantly conduct self-checks. It's like checking in with yourself and then checking in with your love interest. There is so much deception to look out for…you have to make sure that you are being real with yourself and real with others. The "love" feeling is definitely a scary one and a good one at the same time. We have to be able to love openly and accept truth. Enjoy Divine Appointments while they last and learn, learn, learn…and love, love, love…

It Hurts...

Call me emotional, but it hurts when...

You don't call when you say you will...
When you don't return my phone calls...
When you don't text me back...
When you don't make it your business to see me...

It just hurts a little...just a little sting because what I want and what's reality doesn't line up.
It hurts to know that I made some sacrifices all because I wanted to see you and be with you...
But you were too "busy" to notice or care...

It just hurts a little...just a little sting...

When I think about you all day everyday and even see you in my dreams...and still no sign of you.
It hurts because I choose not to make a fool of myself and keep trying to contact you...
It just hurts that I can't even talk to you when I want to...
It hurts because I still don't know you and you still don't know me, yet I gave myself to you...

My body, my mind, my time...and my heart...I felt so connected...started to get that Soulmate feeling...but what did you feel?

I don't know...maybe you thought I was a "joke" or joking...

So it just hurts a little...just a little sting...

What to do when your ego gets bruised?

Firstly, what does this mean? A bruised ago? It is the day you wake up and realize...you may not be "all that" or "he's just not into you". Funny right? But sort of true...I have had a few bruised ego moments...this is when I'm like...last time I checked in the mirror I was fine...thick, pretty in the face, smart...and so on and so forth...one of my wiser friends just recently assured me...it's not you...it's them or "him". I'm like dang...what does a sister have to do these days to get some recognition and reciprocation for all of the hard work and love I put into these relationships? So what to do when the ego gets bruised:

1. Surround yourself with positive people, i.e., girlfriends, guy friends, and family...they will always give you confidence..."saying it's not you it's them" or "such and such is stupid".

2. Check yourself: look in the mirror...make sure you still qualify for being "all that"...if not...start a beauty/health regimen...hit the gym...by a new outfit...change your hair style/color...these things are only temporary but they help.

3. Randomly call, text, or email old lovers/friends of

11

the opposite sex...this is encouraging sometimes... but be careful...do not go down a road that ended poorly...sometimes those ones from 5 to 10 yrs ago make you remember why y'all aren't together and never will be...it's like looking at where you came from...sometimes you can hook back up but...it may only be temporary.

4. Randomly call, text, or email someone you are not really interested in...the "new" guy you gave your contact info to...sometimes it helps, but then you may realize why you haven't given him a chance... but it does stroke the ego.

5. Have sex...okay, really be careful and selective with this one...if you are already emotionally distraught from the bruised ego or guy who kicked you to the curb, this is not always safe...especially if you really like the person who could be from the past #3 or present #4. (I don't particularly encourage one night stands in this day and age...too dangerous...or if you are over the age of 21, i.e. out of college) Also, use caution when going back to a lover from 5 to 10 yrs or someone presently...in the heat of the moment people lose their minds...temporary insanity...want to have unprotected sex...not safe people...we all know this...fear of child out of wedlock should be the least of worries...

6. Get drunk! Again be careful...in your drunkenness... you are susceptible to poor decision-making...i.e. hooking up with past or present love interests that you really are not interested in...cussing out or calling the person who has bruised your ego...

driving by such and such's house...at this point...
you have just become the crazy drunk woman...with
no sense...

7. Okay...so this should have been first on the list...
    but pray...go to church...read your bible...once you
    figure out that the rest of that stuff you tried to do
    to make yourself feel better is only temporary...you
    will realize that the void can only be filled by God...
    it is my hope that filling the void with God and
    His Holy Spirit...will help to heal you and prepare
    you for what is to come...to try and be smarter in
    relationships...to avoid getting a bruised ego...how
    do you do this? Stay in faith...stay focused...weed
    out those being used by the enemy to kill, steal, and
    destroy...

I just don't think that relationships and dating should be
so difficult. Why do people lie? Why don't people keep it real?
Why does a good woman who will do anything for a man
she loves...get dragged through the mud and called "weak"?
So what do you do to be strong? Show no emotion, and no
feelings (like a man)? When will he respect me? When I act
as if I don't care about him? The shit is crazy! The truth is: a
man has to choose a woman...now many times...when or if a
woman chooses a man, it goes nowhere or only so far...what
makes me mad is that when a man does choose a woman...
the test begins...it's like they test us to see how "strong" we
are. We have to be a closed book...can't tell them anything
or only a minimal amount of info regarding the past...it will
always be used against us for him to decide..."naw she ain't
it"...they will use any little thing to disqualify a woman...
once you have been cancelled out in his eyes...you might as
well give it up...the ultimately sad part is that...if you are

fine...with a big booty...he will string you along...until you finally give up on him, he meets the "one" he's been searching for, or you are acting too crazy!

I'm tired of being "that chick"...dragged through the mud...it can't be all my fault...I can't be this stupid...now I'm not ever going to switch sides...but I can see how a woman can become bitter...not ever give any man a chance...or just treat men like ATMs or whatever ya know?...pay before you lay, that type of thing...or just give up dating or even date interracially...(another topic) because no matter the race some of those similarities still remain...

Rejection

What should I do?
Should I cry?
Or Fret?
No.

I must search within.
Only on God can I depend.

He who rejects me,
Is surely not wise.

God said,
I am a light.
And light attracts light.
So therefore, what is not light,
Rejects me!

I am too powerful and bright.
Anything dark cannot handle me.
So I must walk in my light,
And reject what is dark.

Developing a Thick Skin

I swear me having a BIG EGO is not an overstatement! I have to laugh at myself sometimes...LOL! You ever just feel like "I'm the SHIT" so why isn't such and such giving me the play. The truth here is that the such and such I speak of is someone who I never should have given the "play". In an effort to continue whatever we started, I have called and texted. I was successful in my pursuit too...but let's just say that when the night ended, baby I was going home alone...hilarious to me...but it's okay...my Ego, let's call her "Latrece" just for fun and laughs...was hurt, devastated and shocked...not to mention no real companionship in three weeks (if you know what I mean)...almost four now...by choice of course...you know when you choose...you choose because the options are always present...I think...that's Latrece talking again.

I'm going to make this one short...so over the weekend I learned "when it's over it's over". It doesn't matter what you do...if someone is done fooling with you, they are just done...I now understand why Jazmine Sullivan busted the windows out the fella's car...I know how that feels to want to do just that...but watch out for Karma ladies...Have you ever found yourself cussing out someone on his voicemail or sending threatening text messages? With no return calls or texts? OMG...that was me...at the end of the day when you go home and lay it down...turn off your phone and wake up to a new day you realize okay...I'm cool now...I feel better now...everything for a reason. Makes me wanna delete this brother from my phone...I swear...

At the end of the day though...a host of rejection experiences have allowed me to develop a very thick skin... those who know me best know my sensitivities...but I've been through so much now in dating relationships that I'm like... I'm strong enough to withstand almost anything...anything that anyone tries to do to me...shoot has already been done... WOW! I just look back over my young adult life and just don't even know or understand how I made it through...and how I'm still here...still hoping and believing that LOVE is still possible for me!! Let me tell you though...when God is the SOURCE anything is possible...I'm DIVINELY healed as well! Isn't it amazing how God can just allow you to go through the fire and come out shining like pure gold? So I thank and praise Him for that...and am learning to not sweat the small stuff...let my Ego go and know that what's best for me is on the way...so all the JERKS have to be removed... Mr. Right Now can kick rocks!

Eternal Sadness
(Still Waiting...)

Sad...reaching out, won't somebody hear me my lil voice crying out in sorrow only no one hears because I cry from the inside out...smile through the pain, heartache and pain...blood, sweat and tears this agony I feel...alone again, in a crowded room...won't somebody hear...doesn't anybody notice that I'm not really myself...the self that you see...oh, someone please take this pain away...far away, so that I will never have to feel you again...fly away like an Angel... only coming down for short visits...in the wind I hear the Freedom of never feeling this way again...

How many times can a heart break, shake, quake...it is as though it has no protection from the body that covers it...with every tremor, it grows ever more faint...weary is my soul and spirit...still longing for divine connection...a depth that can only be filled by the one who completes...made to love...made for me... my hope is in vain...face filled with shame...wanting to end this misery now and forever...disappear like dust in the wind...only a keen eye can seek, blinded by the light of the darkness within...

Shadows of ill-emotional turmoil...prevail as I try to stay afloat...still perplexed as to how I ended up here in the first place...all alone...without even a friend who does reach out her hand...but it is you I seek continuously...why haven't you found me? Where are you? Please take this pain away...or I shall not live to see another day...without you...

My Own Insecurities

I must confess
I'm a Victim
Yes
Of my own insecurities
The longing of frequently
Needed Validation
Has caused me to
Obsess
Too much, but not enough
Will I ever learn
These situations and things
Are better left to discern
I'm a Victim
Yes, I must confess
Can't you guess?

It's not that easy
To grace the room
With finesse
My own worst enemy
Will I ever change?
Today I try
To make the Exchange

From Victim to Victor!
I overcome
Validation, Justified
By the One...

"You fine, but you a nappy headed mutha fu(c)&a!"

One Friday night, outside of one of StL's hottest night spots, I was approached by an old drunken man; let's call him a "bum" because clearly he wasn't going into the club. This is what he had to say, "You fine, but you a nappy headed mutha fucka"! Can you imagine the look of shock and perplexity on my face after hearing this expression? I was so offended by the ignorance coming from his mouth! I thought, what an idiot...as I continued into the club he further says, "and you a fat (phat) ass"! What? I'm thinking this old drunk ni%%a done lost his mutha fu(c)%in mind!! A lady does not want to hear these comments upon walking into the club... I was more offended by the hair comment than the ass one... So I'm fine and nappy?! Why is he stating the obvious? What was the purpose of his ignorance that night? It is interesting to observe what people will say in or out of the drunken state. So after being at the bar for a little while...another guy, sitting next to me says, "Erykah Baduh". So I just looked at him. He then goes on to say, "no, I like it" (my fro)..."you know she's from Dallas? That's where I'm from". So I told him that I wasn't offended and that I took it as a compliment, but I was waiting to hear what else he was going to say before I said anything. Next, I'm walking by and another guy says "Yeah she got that Jill Scott look" (something to this affect and how some guys like that...and whatever blah blah blah) so I just smiled and kept going. When I passed by him again, I stopped. He goes on to say, "you look like that strong woman who don't need a man"! (He was making references to the independent type of women) I'm looking at him, and I'm responding...and I'm thinking, if this isn't the furthest thing from the truth... Lord I don't know what is! Let's just say that this was a very interesting night...and I didn't even mention this white guy who just couldn't get his drunken words together enough to have a real conversation with me. Every time I looked at him, he appeared dazed, glazed over, and sort of drooling-like (ok, I'm exaggerating a little).

So, I am filling y'all in because...I kept telling my story of the drunk man outside, because I was so offended...and everyone (men and women) were just like whatever...you know you're looking good...and the natural looks nice on you...blasé blasé. So I'm thinking...man this is 2008...why are we, people, defined by our hair? I agree it certainly makes a statement...especially if not fitting in with what is considered to be the norm...How do we define beauty and fineness... etc? Why are Eurocentric ideals of hair straightening so important to us? Just some of the things that have been going through my head...I mean you know India Arie said "I am not my hair"! But...it's crazy how it is such a big deal...

My closest friends know that I have struggled with my self-image for forever now...this whole natural hair thing has become a way for me to accept myself...embrace myself...I told the security people outside the club "This is how God made me"...I mean for real...yes, you can alter this and that and things about yourself...but after a while...think of the maintenance costs...I have even looked at myself on some days...and some pictures like..."ooo, I need a nose job" lol... but for real...once you change one thing...you will always find something else wrong...we, people, need to deal with what is going on inside of us in order to love what it looks like on the outside...I often say sometimes..."we aren't supposed to see ourselves the way other people see us" this works for positives and negatives...sometimes, I look at myself...and I don't see what people see...the beauty...or whatever...but maybe they see the inside that shines through...then too...there are people who may be like "she showl is ugly" lol...but hey...I surely don't need to look at myself like that...what's so funny is that some fine people with ugly ways and attitudes showl is ugly too!

The truth is many of my insecurities come from childhood...my hair was never long enough...I wasn't short enough...I wasn't "light" enough (and I'm not even dark-skinned)...these are the things that can divide or unify black people...one of our blessings is that we all come in different colors and hair textures...in actuality...we are all "others" if you think about it...

Here in lies the need to want to become inseminated by a non-white (black man) of a particular genetic make-up... what a sad an ugly truth...how can one break the chains of feeling as though..."girl, I need a man with some 'good' hair" yeah so that my kids don't go through what I went through... so they can be fine and not nappy headed...just crazy, just foolishness...Wake Up! It's not even about that...love...it shouldn't be...at this rate, I will be blessed with whomever God does send my way. I am definitely a work in progress... just pray for me y'all...if I show up tomorrow with a weave, don't be surprised!

Here's what others had to say about my experience: "How much different would our self-perception be if we saw ourselves through God's eyes?" This is from Rachelle Smith... thanks Rachelle! This is definitely something to think about... like how I told the guys outside..."this is how God made me"... if I keep seeking to alter what He has given...then what's the point? On a lighter note...He sees us as fashioned by His image...I'm going to end with that.

"Good Luv"

Good Luv will make you relocate
Not good sex, good Luv
Have you experienced this?
Good Luv will make you High…
It's good for you, for your Soul…

Distant Lover

I think I'm gaining an understanding of having my heart stolen, captured, and left in another city or cities. Have you ever felt this way? This feeling of wanting to be with someone who is thousands of miles away...It's like being sprung...in one sense, being single means just love locally or date locally or enjoy being with the one or ones who are close to you...but love knows no boundaries...when you love someone or we'll just say extremely like, you want to be with, talk to that person everyday in every way you can... despite boundaries. Do some people shy away from long-distance relationships because of this feeling? Create a sense of detachment out of fear of not being able to get to the one they want to be with. I haven't felt this way in a long time...just giving up the locals for someone distant...how does this happen? I think for women it's easier to give up the locals more so than men, but I may be wrong. "If you can't have the one you love, love the one you're with"...sounds like something a man would say...would you truly be happy in doing so? Or maybe that song actually means, you better love who loves you...but ok, I'm seeking something mutual here...So the other day, I decided to listen to some Marvin Gaye. "Distant Lover" this song explains it all...I mean it sounds like he had a Summer love, and they had to depart from one another. Seasonal lovers...it's like trying to turn a Season into a lifetime. So as we continue to search or not search for love...which in actuality throughout this journey we continuously learn about ourselves; and ultimately if we did not possess that Self-love, find it in the search. Inherently, the lesson is to not give your heart away too soon...some type of trust and understanding of communication should be established first...in situations near or far.

So I am learning, but I also see why it takes some people a long time to trust, love, or give away their hearts. I'm not saying not to love or trust, but when you do love so freely, openly, honestly, everyone is not ready to or doesn't receive it...so you can love by letting them go or developing a sense of detachment...only a detachment that protects yourself but does not hurt others' feelings. It can be a catch 22. The lesson: love yourself...sounds overrated, but it is true...when you love yourself, it doesn't matter what someone does or doesn't do to you or for you. You have already taken care of yourself...

Hmm...in loving someone who is distant or being/acting distant, one may wonder, what is the point of loving or having someone who you can't be with or see or talk to? Again, I guess the point is more so to learn about yourself. There is something called a "love language". We don't all possess the same one. Someone who is acting distant may just have a different love language than you. Okay so that's a positive. In my mind, I'm thinking..."if he doesn't call/text...stalk or etc. everyday, something is wrong with him...should I take a hint...he doesn't love me or let alone like me"...but it's like when we're together...everything is perfect and roses or when we do talk...so there is definitely something off in the communication...or maybe I'm just reading too much into what seems to me like a lack of communication. Now if the stalker was someone that I didn't like, then I'd be annoyed...a catch 22. Kind of a sad situation because I want things to be one way, but in the reality of my mind they are this way...

long distance...not committed...don't talk/text everyday... detached. Again what's the point or purpose?

Maybe I'm void in the department of self-love, which is why I seek an outside source of love...hmmm? Ok, just maybe...maybe I need to re-focus, change my focus. Again, just let this person go...allow them to be free and to communicate their love language to me or not...I've already communicated mine...even if they don't care, don't receive and are not listening. Do I change or alter my love language? Feel bouts of sadness from having withdrawals of him? Find someone else to love? The answer to these questions is NO! Be yourself, cheer up, and love you! Change takes time, but we must work on it everyday. Self-improve...read, work out, stay busy, work on career, hang out with family and friends, date others (if you're feeling up to it)...there's a lot to do while sitting around waiting for the one you love to call...the one who already knows how you feel about him...I am not one to hide my feelings, but I can't control what someone does with that info. I don't know his reaction. He says that the feelings are mutual, but I don't see that in his actions.

Again, I'm learning...more so about me than anything or anyone else...my aim is to be free from all of my anxieties...to get through this process and come out loving myself more... knowing myself best...expecting the best in life and from others...but also with the reality that things happen; and that I can't change someone and that regardless of what I do or say, people are going to be and do themselves anyway with or without my love. Right now, I'm reluctant to start anything new or rekindle anything old. I'm not up for it. I just want to do me...and work on me...I know that I've fallen in love with someone...but is it really love...okay so I won't say in love, but that I do love someone...again though..."if it isn't love, then say what it is"...another song. Seriously, it may feel like love, but it could be infatuation...the opposite would

be unconditional love which involves the ability of sacrifice…
would I give this person a lung…an arm…a kidney…whoa!
So maybe it's not love…it's a good feeling, but not when
it's not reciprocated the way I expect it. So I would like to
see where these feelings lead me with this person…maybe
it will just be "history" or something to go in the "friend"
file…which is okay with me right now. It hurts a little…but
who said that growing had to feel good…I know that I will
look back on these experiences a changed woman…a "grown"
woman…a wise woman…and someone who is at peace about
my life for choosing to not harden my heart despite what
people do or don't do.

"Love is a Choice. Lust is an addictive Desire. Infatuation
is Foolish. Sometimes all three collide in our perception of
someone". –Dr. Rae

What Makes a Man?

Is it his hands?
His eyes
His lips
His shoulders

What Makes a Man?
Is it his brain?
His money
His attitude
His walk

What he thinks makes a man
And what I think makes a man don't compare
A man keeps it real with me at all times
Even when it hurts
Because he knows the truth will set us free

A man does not just look at me and think sex
He thinks beauty
And when we make love
He seeks to please me

A man takes care of me and his children
He almost never comes first
This is what makes a man
He is your brother, your father, your lover, and your friend
This is what makes a man

He works hard
He hustles
He protects
This is what he was born to do

Have High Standards

"Have high standards...and they will be there."
--K.K.P. (2009)

In regard to dating...You never know what people have been through...my co-worker age 35 recently revealed to me that she was married twice before marrying her current Husband. Prior to me knowing this about her, I thought... wow...she has it all...married to a Professor...baby on the way...working on her Doctorate...You Go Girl...me looking through envious eyes...and especially on the days that I drank my hater-aide...

But now I'm thinking...you never know what people have been through...abuse...mean men...men focused more on themselves than you...the list is endless...My co-worker said now she has no complaints...Hubby number 3 is "perfect"...I said well, "I pray for a Husband like that". She said that she did. I told her that she is blessed...and that's when she revealed the history of her failed relationships.

So I asked her for some advice and she simply said, "Have high standards...and they will be there." I mean this simple sentence put some things into perspective for me...It just means don't settle...stop doing all the bending...and thinking that something is wrong with you...No commitment...tell him to kick rocks! But for real...maybe "he's just not that into you"...

But someone else surely will come along...I mean...as long as you believe...and realize that you are too smart to deal with someone who treats you like you're worthless...

Part II
Reality Check: Wake Up!

I Am Woman Enough

I am woman enough
To be your lady
I'm strong, bright, black, and beautiful
I miss you
This distant companionship we share
I am woman enough
To realize I care
What a mystery?
As I remember looking into your eyes
So much man
I'm so hypnotized
What is the truth?
That I need to see
Or will it always remain a mystery?

I was just thinking...is dating getting better as I age? I say yes! Sure I've had those days of reflection, and I think that I should have been married or had children by now, but there comes a time when most individuals unmarried especially reach a point or let's call it a plateau. There is a point where a person feels like "whatever happens happens". Not to thwart your heart's desires or plans, but this type of attitude gives a person more patience while waiting for their Mr. or Ms. Right. As I approach my 29th birthday, (so old right? just kidding) I now finally understand what everyone says when they say, oh just wait and/or just keep working on yourself, just keep on loving yourself. Hey, it finally all makes sense. All those horrible clichés no one wants to hear when they are in search of their Mr. Right. You know I've heard it all. Focus on yourself; find out what you like...blah, blah, blah. The reality is that these sayings are so true. I've even heard, "how can you truly love someone else if you don't completely love yourself?" I have to admit that one never really made sense to me because don't we all have the ability to love ourselves and others? But what that means is like on an airplane; they tell you to make sure you have your oxygen mask on first before you start trying to help those surrounding you. Okay, I love that analogy. How can I love on someone else if I dislike everything about me? And when you really love yourself, others can't help but see what you see or feel the vibrations you give off. And if they don't see what you see then you know what I always say "kick rocks" chump!! Lol!

But yes, my outlook on dating is definitely becoming better as I age; and as I continue to work on and love me. Like fine wine baby. How long does it take to get to this point? It is different for everyone. Not to be egotistical, but just to really develop an attitude of accepting nothing but the best from the people in your life or whom you date. It may take some people to have children before they reach this point or to encounter divorce. Some get this while they're still young, others long after 30, and maybe some never get it. But it is a beautiful feeling to possess; just being happy with yourself and still expecting to attract a wonderful Mate. When you and your potential Mate are both at this point in life, you can do nothing but make beautiful music together. You both realize your own worth, each others' worth, and that you both deserve the best out of life and from each other. There is nothing like having this mutual respect and the union will be blessed.

Furthermore, on this plateau, some have discovered that being married is not part of their life's purpose. They have become very content with themselves or their work. They may realize that they don't want to have children or be married, but possibly still date people or just one person. There is nothing wrong with this because married life isn't for everyone. The key is to make sure that you are happy with your life whatever path you choose.

Is it okay?

Is it okay that some days I'm not feeling myself?
Is it okay that some days I fear losing you?
Is it okay that some days I feel like I'm dreaming?
Is it okay that some days I don't trust you?
Is it okay that some days I don't feel I deserve your love?
Is it okay that I'm like this because of my past hurts?
Is it okay that you may have to work extra hard to get me to believe in us?

Tell me is it okay?

Is it okay that I think I'm in love with you?
Is it okay that I want to move away from my present to be in your presence?
Is it okay that I want to be with you?
Is it okay that I dream about you in the day and night?
Is it okay that I can see myself being your wife?

Tell me is it okay?

Digital Love

Has technology enhanced or complicated
our love and dating relationships?

*N*ow this is a topic I have wanted to discuss for some time. When you hear the phrase "Digital Love", what do you automatically think? E-harmony? Match.com? Facebook? Myspace? Online dating...Internet dating...the virtual hook-up...well whatever you think of, it's all the same. Do you really think that people are "networking" on myspace and facebook? (Some are...either that or being nosy, trying to see what past lovers are up to and if he or she is married/in a relationship what have you) That's just something you say when you don't want to seem desperate for a date..."networking". Yeah, I'm making some assumptions here. Anyway, how is the digital environment affecting the dating scene? I will tell you my thoughts, and then let me know what you think.

I think online dating/mating is and can be fun. Yes, I've tried it, "networking"! If you've never met the person before, it can be a little scary, especially upon the first meeting. You don't know what to expect, and you pray that the person is really who they say they are or the same person as the picture on their profile. Beware of people who try to "holla" who don't post a picture at all. I don't think anyone is that silly, but you never know. If you are meeting someone you met online for the first time in person, please bring a friend...and try not to just make it a "hook-up" unless that's just what you are on (protect yourself).

Some of the benefits of the digital love world include e-mail, texting, instant messaging, and video/camera phones and web cams (I don't have one of those), these amenities aid in keeping in touch especially for long-distance relationships. Yes, we've come along way from the pen-pal method. This works if you met the person out and about or online. The only disadvantage is that sometimes these methods can replace the need for "real" time or even just time on the phone. Believe you me, "there is nothing like the real thing baby" so the little cute daily texts and e-mails are enough to sustain you while you're at work or doing whatever it is that you do. When it's all said and done though, these ways of communicating get you ready for the real time. Do you agree?

In reality, some relationships need not go any further than digital. Sometimes it's just flirting...but when signals get crossed it can become hazardous...I mean you could really be feeling a person, but do you really know them if you've never really spent time with them or even talked to them on the phone? The digital world does help us with our busy schedules. Sometimes it's just easier to drop a quick e-mail than actually spend time on the phone. This type of communication has turned me into a non-phone person. When it comes down to it, dating digitally or physically is just like this song my girl always sings "if your heart isn't in it..." But it's true..."where your treasure (time, money... emphasis mine) is, there also will your heart be" (Matthew 6:21). So what are you making an investment in? Are you really just networking and having fun, or are you really trying to get to know someone? Or just making an online booty call? Regardless of your dating methods, the intentions of your heart will be revealed.

My Drug

Can I bottle you up...?
I told you I been high all day...just the thought of you...
I don't wanna mess this up...if so, lesson learned...
So much I wanna say...so much I wanna be...but we gotta move slowly

Time always reveals truth
So what did you come to do?
Not to just ease my pain, but to heal...
It's a journey...it's been a long road...
And this is just the beginning

So let's go to a different level...
What can I be for you?
What do you need from me?
I'm open...
To have love...one must be love...and love

Without limits...without restrictions...
Unconditionally...
Desperate...No...that's not me...
Just made to love.

Right now, at this present moment...
I choose you...
I'm jonesin'...as they call it...

I love feelin' this way...
I must be in love with love...

Let me learn how to love you,
And you do the same for me.
We're in control...
You know what I'm feelin', and I can't fight it
Hooked on you...addicted to your energy within...
My temporary high...my drug...

Love Is Everywhere
(and God is Love)

*H*ave you checked your love bank account today? Is it full or empty? Do you need more love in your life? Well if you look around you, love is everywhere! Love within or Self-love, love from God, love from family, love from friends, love from animals. You see what I mean? Love is everywhere! If you are ever feeling depleted in this area, or maybe suffering from insufficient love funds, just take a look around. If you still don't see the love or feel the love, how much love are you giving? What you give will be given unto you. I firmly believe in this principle. It may not come to you from the person who you are giving it to, but it will come or is already present. You deserve love; especially God's love. How can you live without love? Remember, love is everywhere and God is love. Love is within you. So give give give love and you will have a full love account, and will receive so much love in return! Just look for the love. Sometimes it can become overwhelming, but we are all in this cycle together. The person who you love so dearly that may not be reciprocating in a way familiar to you or in the way that you give, should not be deleted from your love cycle (unless it becomes too emotionally unstable). As you give to this person, you may receive many surprises along the way and/or secret admirers; people or persons you would not even notice or choose to love. So the love always comes back to you. I am speaking from experience. How can you not love someone who loves you? Someone who is so endearing toward you? You may decide that I just don't love this person the same way he or she loves me. It is clear to set some sort of boundaries so that you are not leading a person on into thinking that the relationship is more than what it is. Hopefully, you and the person can come to some type of terms for what the relationship means for the two of you. Words unspoken can be very hurtful.

So to keep the good karma coming in, try your best to establish love boundaries. Receive the love and reciprocate the best way you know how. Being in love and/or loving is a beautiful thing! Fill up your love account today!

The Focus

Falling in love is not the focus...not right now...my life purpose is way more important. It is my hope that you will become a part of my purpose...but you are not the focus...the focus is me...my Creator...my destiny...my duty... what's your focus?...my focus is to love...me and you...and what I do...one thing at a time...let's fall in line...together... let's love...let's share...let's make a difference in the world... together or apart...you are in my heart...but not my main focus...I do love you...but I do love me...and who I am to be in this world...friends' love last longer than lovers' anyway... you're my lover and my friend...let's focus on being friends right now...we'll have plenty of time to make love...when the work is done...I'm working on me and you're working on you...what a blessing to still have a heart connection without the stress...we have mutual understanding and respect... no better feeling between the two...just focus...see what I see...the big picture...the symphony sounds better once each individual note has been mastered...if I don't do my part and you don't do yours...our music will not blend...it will end in discord...we've both been there before...so right now I'll just focus on mastering me instead of seeking to manipulate you to give me what I need...I give to myself...I receive what you give...I allow you the freedom to be you...and I freely give to you too...

Preoccupied Women Find Love

So...I was inspired today at work by one of my co-workers...y'all know I love love...so she was telling me about how she met her Husband. How many times have we heard "don't look for love", or "it will happen when you're busy and not thinking about it"? Well basically she was saying that she had given up on finding or being found by love. Her mom told her that she wasn't gonna find it sitting at home on the couch...lol...true though. So she got a second job. Sista girl became very consumed with work (life). So her co-workers at her second job (part time), a fun job at a drive-in theater, kept hooking her up on blind dates with their relatives...let's just say, the third time was a charm. She said the first two were "putz"...I think that's the word she used. She went on to say that all her life she has struggled with her weight and her size. After getting married, she gained more weight; which she said she wasn't going to do. But guess what? Her Hubby loves her despite how she feels about herself...she said when they were dating...and Hubby is a hearty eater (a country boy who loves fried food)...all he wanted to do was go out to eat...so imagine how she felt...on a diet and on a date...Go figure! She said that he told her he just loves her the way she is. Amazing! This is how it should be.

Ladies, stay busy! How many times have I, Raechel Rivers, heard this advice and not taken heed to it? In my mind somehow I conjured up that if I don't "look", I won't find…so not true and so pessimistic. The truth is life is too short to only focus on this one aspect. There is so much about life to be discovered and enjoyed; and this should be done before we leave this earth. Our days are numbered and we don't know how many we have. I'm convinced that I just want to be happy…single or married…I want to enjoy my life in spite of;…life should be good…because what if you got a spouse and the day after you married he died or was in a car wreck? How devastating would that be to have to endure something like that after waiting so long to get a spouse? Michelle McKinney Hammond says in her books "live life as though you will never get married". Yes, that's a hard pill to swallow…I'm telling you I didn't want this advice at 25 heck; not even last year!

But God has a special purpose and plan for each of us… and it is good! He knows our heart's desires…but He also knows what's best. How many wives or divorced people do you know who have said they were so young when they married that they didn't know what they wanted from life or that they liked certain things? I think it's beautiful when a couple can be together forever and grow and learn new things together instead of growing apart, but it doesn't always work that way for everyone. Saying all of that to say, find out what makes you happy…"do you"…"and the rest of these things shall be added unto you" (Matthew 6:33). This is easier for me to say at 29 than at 25…but I want the "best" for my life…"no more jerks"…"no more playas". Even if I have to be "asexual" as my "Twin" would say. I mean why settle? Settling (sin)…is only for a season…obedience brings the blessing. I want to be blessed not cursed in all that I do. So I don't need to share my body or my time with "Joe" if he is not my Husband ordained by God.

Again stay busy…what man doesn't like an unavailable woman? (They have been designed to "chase" to hunt (the nature of the beast). Shoot I'm the same way...have fallen really hard for some unattainable jerks...and that was a life lesson, but a waste of time and energy...I could have been working on becoming a Superstar or a Millionaire the time I spent chasing. (It was the law of attraction (distraction). So hey...just work on you...pursue your dreams because before you know it...you'll be pushing 40 still on the phone with your girlfriends bashing men...and I'd rather be somewhere vacationing in Jamaica...ya know? And another thing, I love my girlfriends, but I know we get tired of having to be each other's shoulder to cry on when it doesn't work out...time out for that...let's just be happy...Love yourself!! More importantly Love God because He will never leave you nor forsake you...if only you believe...and you can rest in that!

Textin'
(3:18 a.m.)

Some things just aren't meant to be. Maybe one day. I wanted to be the one but you didn't choose me. I keep wondering why? I'm tired of this fight. Is it all in vain? Why do I feel like a fool for thinkin' you and me could have been? When you ain't changin' or lettin' me in. A fool for you. I still have my dignity. Where are you? Why you not here with me? Everything is fucked up now. That's all she wrote. The fat lady sang. The deaf man spoke. There's more to me than what you see. You so blind you see what you want. What about the woman made to love. You wasn't ready and now she's gone. I'm out waitin' for you to reciprocate but you been pre-programmed to set up a wall... she feels that you can't love her like she needs. Soul crying out desperately seeking the man who heals. This is love she feels. But you won't let me love you...

"Love, Lies, Lames"

1) Love

Have you ever met someone and you were just like dang, he or she (for my guys) is my Soulmate. You were able to see the potential of this relationship. You actually had a few interactions with this person (no, not just on Facebook). Okay, because you didn't meet this person on Facebook. So in the beginning...you were feeling like you were feeling. You thought this person was feeling the same way...just by the few phone conversations, e-mails, and texts. You felt like everything was all good with this person, not a whole lot of drama or what not. You even asked this person (just to be on the safe side) if they were "involved" with someone or had a girlfriend/boyfriend. And the answer was always "No"... you would ask this person, "do you like me"? (again to protect your heart because no one likes to get played). And then one day...hear it comes...BAM!! A woman or a man (guys probably can't relate to this) contacts you out of the blue like please don't contact my man. WTF? What would you have done in this situation? I'll tell you what I did...I went off on her and the guy. 1. He said that he didn't have a girlfriend, and 2. A grown woman who is secure within her relationship has no business contacting another woman about a man who is obviously lying about being with her. In the end, I was left feeling like a "fool" because of someone else's deception and inability to keep it real with me. Now the sucka is treating me like I did something wrong?! I say the crap just blew up in his face! I'm glad that I now know the TRUTH, but I'm upset that the dude didn't just tell me the truth from the beginning. I then would not have been so "in love".

2) Lies

Why do people lie? What a perverse generation we live in filled with greed, deception, and lies. "If I were a boy..." Hmmm...what do y'all think that would be like? Would I be good or bad? Anywho, I just have a difficult time respecting LIARS! My tolerance is minimal to none. Yes, there were plenty of red flags, but when you have the rose-colored glasses on you see what you want. Okay, I'm guilty. I'm guilty of expecting the good in people. Me, let me check myself... have I always kept it 100? I most definitely try...if I'm not "into" someone, they will know it...on the other hand if I am, then they will know it. I'm just saying, who wants to or has time to play the guessing game at this age when it comes to dating and relationships. I'm starting to believe that it was so much better 10-12 years ago. Sure we've all had our ups and downs in relationships and they've made us who we are... but geesh...when do you reach the dating plateau...climbing this mountain can't always be this difficult. Speaking of mountains, many of us may not make it to the top...some of us are really just tired. Our lack of strength or will to keep climbing can cause apathy, lethargy, etc...I mean seriously... the whole "just do you"...eh...worst advice. I understand the concept, but it seems that everyone is doing themselves (lol)...having their cake and eating it too! And where does this lead you? Some of us have "settled"...and many of us are beginning to give up.

3) Lames

Not much to say about what a lame is: a scrub, a liar,

a fool! Someone who thinks he is or wants to be a playa! Someone who is endangering the lives of himself or others sexually. Someone who just doesn't keep it real. I say that good things are not going to come to someone who is living his or her life based on lies and deceit. I don't understand how someone can sleep at night knowing that he or she is lying to everyone they know. Sleeping with multiple people and still not being real with their own person. That's right just LAME! Please don't be guilty of falling in love with a lame person. Someone who is running from the truth. To me, a real player is someone who can be accountable to and confess his or her actions. They just keep it real. When you meet this person, they tell you…"this is what it is and this is what it ain't…and this is what it ain't gonna be". They don't lead you into believing that you are the one for them or that they could see y'all being together. BLAH BLAH! Right?! A player will tell you what you are getting yourself into…How many real players do you know? I can only think of maybe 3. People want to run around lying to themselves. People want what they want from you and will go to many lengths to get what they want from you; be it money, sex, time, food, whatever, whatever, the list goes on…

In conclusion, I have had to learn the hard way the nature of the "beast". So as we climb this mountain, let's take off the rose-colored glasses. Let's get down to the business of weeding out the wolves from the sheep. Because the wolf is no joke! He will have you out here looking crazy and your bank account empty. I'm just saying…it's so hard out here for a player…being Single doesn't sound so bad after all. Karma is a mutha…so just be sure that what you are putting out is good because it comes back 10-fold. I'm resting on the fact that "vengeance is the Lord's"…no good thing will He withhold from those who walk uprightly. So hey, I keep it real and I expect my "future" mate to be just as real as me!

Part III
A Work in Progress: Learning

I'm Ready...Are You?

Are you ready for all of me?
That decision is major
Do you know what's ahead in dealing with me?
Playtime is over babe
If you hadn't realized, I'm not average
Or Petite in size

You have to be ready for ALL this woman
She's sassy, classy, and every bit of jazzy!
She's spiritual, emotional, and an intellectual
She's in tune with herself and her world
So tell me, are you ready?

My time is precious
I'll make room for you in my world
If you do the same
Tell me are you willing to sacrifice
The time it takes to really get to know me?
I'm ready...are you?

April 10, 2010

The Journey...to Self...

Your girl has been undergoing some major changes this year...all for the better. Working on finishing my Doctoral Program; defining what truly makes me happy and so on and so forth. 2010 hasn't been glorious...but many of the changes are occurring within, which are going to bring me into a better state mentally, physically, emotionally, and spiritually. My "Love" writing seems to have taken a backseat. Actually, this is not true. I am truly embracing what this whole Self-love thing is about. Me and my Sistas have really become worn out of the whole "can't get this Man thing right" topic; but really, is it them or is it us that's the problem? I'm concluding that it's a combination of the two. We as women truly need to stop thinking that we need a man to validate us! Uh oh...stepping on my own toes. Let me explain...you may be thinking, Rae what are you talking about? I don't believe that! The truth is that our "need" for a man...a good man... is okay and natural. I think that the need to feel validated comes across in how we act and react to our situations with our men.

For example, we are defined by so many things on a regular basis, like our hairstyles; the way we dress; our occupations; who or how many men we've dated in the past; our children; our cars; etc. You feel what I'm saying? So the type of man that we desire or who we see ourselves with in fact validates us; but this should not be the case. I always tell my friends, I've tried all types of men. From the college/ Master degree educated to the preacher to the comedian to the just barely made it out of high school. You feel me? Often times, I struggle in conversations with people because they feel that just because I'm working on an advanced degree that I should be with a man who has one or what have you. For me, that is the furthest thing from the truth...which you must define your own self-truths, and don't let anyone tell you who you are.

There is more to me than my 2.75 degrees...the man who can realize that about me will have to be the "chosen One". There are men that I know who minimize my educational attainment; it's almost never discussed. Then there are some who...my word...that's all they're interested in about me...I'm just like look...there is so much about me than what meets the eye. I'm sure that you, my Sisters, can definitely relate to this. For example, you may feel like there is more to you than just a pretty face, or big boobs or booty, and there truly is...

We are God's precious creations...do we know how precious we are? Do our men know this as well? Now for the Sistas...society has beaten us up so much...as well as raised us up in certain lights. Sometimes our men feel that they can't compete. I am living for the day when Sistas and Brothas can just love each other instead of always having to compete with status...maybe then can we truly come into some loving drama-free relationships. Relationships where there won't be so many questions regarding sexuality and infidelity. True love; not loving a man or woman because of his or her car or degrees or bank account, but just love. Few of us are finding it...but we must know that it starts with self.

I'm on this journey of finding me...knowing that true love and the things that I truly desire in a Mate are on the way... and you know we have to be ready in order to truly recognize it...I thought I was ready...but actually...I'm not...I'm still in the process of defining what's really important to me. Someone who validates me because of his stature/status/looks? Or someone who has the heart? Both would be nice. God will reveal...in exactly the right time...and this I know...for now...there's so much to do just to get and keep Rae right! And don't waste time with anymore jerks that are going to drain you mentally, physically, emotionally, and spiritually...the world is already doing that enough!

Be Woman Enough

Be Woman Enough to Know what you want out of Life...
Be Woman Enough to Know what you want from a Man
Be woman enough to know when a relationship
or friendship has run its course
Be woman enough to go get what you want
Be woman enough to Let Go...
Be woman enough to Trust God
Be woman enough not to settle in Life or Love
Be Woman Enough to Know Who You Are
Be Woman Enough to Be You!

Lessons: Yesterday Is the Past

*L*ife is filled with learning lessons. How do we learn from yesterday? Some situations in life may have left us feeling brokenhearted. Maybe the man or woman you were interested in hasn't given you the time of day. Maybe you didn't get that dream job for which you applied. Regardless of the result of the circumstances, there was something possibly challenging that you had to learn. It may have left you wondering, "why me?" "Why are things not turning out the way I intended?" Especially when dealing with people; there may be so much mis-communication involved. I for one consider myself to be a top communicator, but maybe I've failed a few times in this department without even realizing it.

Sometimes life will present us with opportunities to really evaluate ourselves and our actions through our dealings with others. You may encounter someone who treats you poorly for no reason that you can apparently see. Even when you try to get to the bottom of their actions or inactions, you may still come up without a conclusion. This outcome really makes you investigate yourself. You start to question what you did to cause the person to treat you badly. Many questions; you begin to place the blame on yourself for their behavior toward you. Two things could be happening: 1) The person may really have a personal problem or even just difficulty communicating; or 2) The lesson may be for you to recognize how you've possibly mistreated someone.

Whatever the case, sometimes as we go through the emotions of hurt and anger, we want to do things to hurt the person who has caused us heartache. When there is no communication, there is no understanding on your behalf as to why the person is choosing to diminish your relationship. Instead of seeking to harm this person, it's best to just let go of your anger and hurt. The only person that anger and hurt are harming is in fact you. When we are weighed down by situations of the past, yes even yesterday, 24 hours ago, it keeps us from moving forward in life. Take the lesson as just that. Learn from it! The next time you are presented with something similar or someone similar, you will know just how to act.

Everything must run its course in life. If someone has been selling you a dream about a relationship, or possible relationship, the truth will always come out based on their actions. Always seek the truth when dealing with unknown outcomes. If a relationship situation does not present itself in the way you desire, it's best to move on. If you've been "talking to", casually dating, booty calling, or whatever your definition of dating is these days, for years and years with a person, without any change or serious commitment, it's time to let go. If the state of the situation is not what you desire, let go. Why hold on to something that does not appear to have any growth?

Again, sometimes we aren't ready to let go of an ideal that we've created in our heads about a situation. I know that things change and people can change too, but how much time of your precious life are you willing to sacrifice of not being completely happy? How long does it take for us to realize that a situation just is what it is and it's not going anywhere? 3 months, 6 months, 1 year, 3 years, 6 years, or 10? Sure it was fun while it lasted. There was so much to learn along the way, but at some point, if it doesn't look like what you desire, you have to release it. Hopefully sooner than later; if not, the lesson will intensify with even more heartache and pain. Let's work on leaving yesterday in the past. Forgive the person for their actions and look forward to a brighter future with someone else or achieving something that will truly make you happy in life!

"Transformation"

It's not easy to embrace
This transitional phase
All around me things are changing
Or is it just me
My Perspective
My Perceptions
Of my world
And me
Deciding who I am
And who I long to be
This never-ending journey
Of Self-Discovery
Tearing down the walls and images I see
Media telling me who I need to be
Transformation takes time,
Effort, growth, change
Longing for my surroundings and circumstances
To change
But all I can control is me
My Destiny
Embracing me
Loving me
Just the way I am
The way I present myself to you
This is me

The real me you wanted to see
Unaltered by the society I see
Starting over
Getting back to the root
To the heart
Transforming Continuously
From the start...

Detox Your Body; Detox Your Life
(May 2010)

You want to know what happens when you detox? You SHIT!! Literally, the more good foods you put in (and not simultaneously with the bad foods), the more the bad stuff, built up fecal matter, comes out. Thank God!! You have to expel all the old shit from your body. All of the negative things and energy that are holding you back. Old habits and ways of thinking. Past relationships, etc, etc,. It's not just about losing pounds, but it's also about losing baggage, and dead weight. A lifestyle change. These are some of the things that are weighing us down and possibly keeping us from moving forward in life. You are changing your mental habits by realizing that all the crap you were addicted to was weighing you down and that all the good food, fruits, veggies, and nuts (mostly raw) uncooked will lead you to a healthier happier you. It's worth the investment. It's worth releasing the caffeine, sugar, and or alcohol addiction; that some may not even recognize as an addiction. I don't want anything that's harmful for me in the long run to have any power over me.

Sometimes we even get addicted to relationships that are unhealthful for us. So as we detox we release the baggage we gained as a result of some of these relationship situations. How can you expect your Soulmate to find you if you are not you? You are walking around full of shit! Literally…all the meat, all the sugar, all the caffeine, all the liquor that is weighing you down. You have become addicted to these things for various reasons; some of them are comfort foods. They taste good going down, but in the long run the only benefits will be an extra fat tush. Nothing against fat booties, but honestly, our fat booties have been known to catch a man but not necessarily keep one. Do you hear me?

I am a woman on a mission to get my mind, body, and spirit back in its true order; in the Divine Order which God has called it to be. Ladies our health, mental, spiritual, emotional, and physical should be top priority! When you are in your best condition, complete, healthy, and whole in mind, body, and spirit, you can attract the same type of mate. Likewise, when you are walking around full of shit, you will also attract some shitty men. I'm tired of the shitty men! So it has to begin with me. As you begin to take care of yourself, and rise to your new level of health, you will notice the shit begins to cease. As you detox yourself, certain men will not even be on your level. Why? You know the answer, they are full of it and you are not. You will be able to recognize the early warning signs because your body and mind will be clear and receptive to a "shit talker". You will probably be able to smell the shit!

I'm on Day 4 of my detox. I'm very proud of myself too. I see my end result now. We have to "begin with the end in mind". I have 5 months before I'm 30 and I see myself emerging as a new and rare creature in body, mind, and spirit. Not necessarily untouchable, but on my new level; my grown woman. Still seeking to be found by the "one", but while I "wait" there is no better feeling than working on me! Ladies, release the shit TODAY! (Smile, because I love you.)

Oh, I almost forgot to add, my overall goal for the 5 months is at least 20lbs. Over the past 4 and a half years of pursuing a Ph.D. and a love life (chasing the wrong things, shitty men), I've accumulated some bags; saddle bags; hail damage what have you. I realized that I'm too young for this. So now I'm working to release an overall gain of 40lbs! Wow! That's 10lbs per year. I'm down 20lbs right now. Just think, all that I went through just in the past four years, now has to be reversed, and I'm okay with this. I'm actually enjoying the journey to the new me. (No more late night Krispy Kremes; no more entire bottles of wine in one night; no more late night McDonald's; etc.)

What type of bags have you been accumulating? What do you need to release in order to reach your desired state or attract a healthy mate? I don't think this goal of attracting a mate is unreasonable. I believe he's out there. The first step is to believe. The second is to become the best you! And always trust God to work things out for your highest good!

The Woman in the Mirror

Who is this woman I see in my mirror? I greet her everyday whether I want to or not. Have I really taken a good look at her lately? Who is she to herself? Who is she to the world? What really matters to this woman? I have watched her evolve from a little girl to a woman…yet I still see her innocence. From awkward to beautiful…from clumsy to graceful…she is becoming and coming into her True Self and person. Her Spirit shines as brightly as the little girl she once knew. Who is this woman in the mirror? She has embraced all of her flaws. She is a constant work in progress. She lives without guilt or regret. She knows that even her mistakes along life's journey have made her into the beautiful creature standing before her. She sees herself as Godly. She knows her worth! God has not given her the Spirit of Fear. She is Love! Every step she takes and every breath she breathes is bringing her closer to her Destiny and Divine Self. The cares of this world have no Power over her Life! She is the Creator of her Happiness and Success! Every person she meets knows that she is a Vessel to be used by God. Her Vibration of the Divine is so High that no lower vibrations can survive within her presence. She is God ordained to produce great works! She knows who she is and whose she is. Her Energy and Light permeate this Earthly realm. She possesses the Feminine energy to nurture and heal as well as the Masculine energy to direct and lead. This woman in the mirror is from God and operates as such!

Wisdom & Understanding: The Epiphany

*L*ast week was a little rough. I had been praying about a certain situation with a guy; praying for some type of revelation as to why this man stopped communicating with me. Now, I began my detox program on May 1, 2010. As you know with the detox, you do more than shed the physical pounds; you also shed the dead weight; i.e., jobs, people, old thoughts and habits from your life. Somehow, it's just difficult to go backwards when you begin the journey to your Higher Self. Reverting back will always make this difficult and painful for you because as a result you will have to undo and redo everything you've been working toward so diligently; the ultimate lifestyle change.

The turmoil I experienced this past week was not in vain. Thank God! I just received the revelation that I had been praying for as well as my healing. As you know, the process had already begun prior to making contact with the man who has decided to become (M.I.A.) missing in action from my life. I also deviated from my new, pure and holistic diet, which may have clouded my judgment. Let's just say, when you are on your way to your next level and to your healing, do not seek out behaviors, individuals, or anything that will be harmful to you. Sometimes you will not be aware of whether or not a certain person in your life is possibly toxic. Your Higher Self is always communicating what's best for you 24/7, but you really have to listen and pay attention. Often times, the universe (God), is actually doing us a big favor when someone decides to exit our life without giving us a warning sign.

Presently, I'm totally okay now with the recent rejection I've encountered. It has brought me back to my life's mission. Now that I've re-focused my energy back on developing things that I love (my work, my writing), I feel 100% better. I can't believe that I allowed myself to travel backwards on my journey. So for the last week, I was really trying to figure out what went wrong? Why ol' boy has just disappeared on me? But some type of miraculous healing has taken place in my life, and it took seven whole days and also getting back to my pure diet for me to receive this healing. I mean I had been beating myself up thinking I did something wrong to run the brother away. The more he ignored me, the more the crazy woman, old me acted out. Acting out is never the way to get a man's attention. He will come around when he's good and ready; I just don't know what the excuse for no communication will be and honestly I could care less. My being able to look back on even my past year of development of self is enough for me to be proud of and realize how strong I really am.

Anyone who appears to try and drag you down or get you off of your path to the ultimate love of self and Creator doesn't need to be around anyway. Those are people who only want to be around for their own self-interests and not to add any type of substance to your life. It is better to recognize the red flags early on; and you know what, the flags were present the whole time. I just ignored them and pursued what I thought would be satisfying for me at the time. In the long run, I wound up feeling hurt and misunderstood. I'm so grateful and thankful for this day to be able to wake up and worry no more about a week old situation. Letting go and focusing on me has been the best remedy thus far!

Pretty Girls

These days it seems that being pretty just isn't enough
Wanna know how I know?
Because all the ugly girls got a man!
Pretty was pretty enough to catch him,
But certainly not keep him...
So what is pretty anyway?
Is he scared of the pretty lady?
Intimidated perhaps?

There used to be a day when she could walk into a room
And men would fall to their knees
Praising the beautiful sight to see
With all this glory and admiration
What keeps her single?

Pretty is what pretty does...

Pretty doesn't really want a man...
Pretty thrives on the words of many
And this is what she'll be...
A work of art for all to see
She's pretty...

And that's how it shall always be...

(to be continued...)

Sex and the City 2: Less is Sometimes Best

This movie had some very important relationship and "relations" themes that we've possibly lost in our Westernized society. Now some of the practices of Eastern culture are way extreme, but we can learn from the ideal of minimizing lustful situations. In actuality these situations can be created from "covering up", but letting it all hang out too soon can also create an adverse affect amongst men and women; such as a man's decision to view a woman as a harlot versus seeing her as the covered up "Virgin Mary".

So what is truly sexier to men? Booties and breasts hanging out, or the woman who a man has to ponder in his mind about? "Hmm…I wonder what she looks like under there?"; ie her clothes or head wrap. "Her eyes are beautiful… so I wonder how beautiful the rest of her body is?" The practice of covering up commands a certain respect from a man, and he doesn't want other men to see or have his prize or goods. In turn, not knowing what her ASSets look like will drive the man wild, like a little boy who imagines and dreams. This man will have the drive to find out all about this woman.

The positive for women is that the man is forced to find out about her mind without lusting for her before the wraps are taken off. At times, all our accessories can be a distraction and seek to define us. Yes even our hair! (in reference to the movie "Good Hair"). These superficial maintenance ideals could possibly keep men from truly getting to know us. I for one like all women of every culture (as portrayed in the movie), love getting "dolled up", and our men enjoy seeing us happy. However, they, if they are a straight man, could care less about how much our clothes cost; what designer we're wearing; what hairstyle we have; how much our nails and massage cost; or how long it took to get done; unless we are "wifey" and it then affects their bank account.

They love us for us...well, a real man does. They love us for our minds; when we're all dolled up or when we are just taking it easy in some sweats and a scarf. Remember what Drake said; "that's when you're the prettiest, I'm hoping you don't take it wrong". Men tell me, that we women dress up for each other. There's some truth in that. Now the shallow men are different. If they see you in the club with your headwrap they may look the other way. However, confidence and beauty are within. I've gone from the fro, to braids, to the long weave, to the "Halle" cut, to the headwrap, and still have no problem pullin 'em. (But I'm a real life chameleon).

The strength in being a chameleon is that its power involves the ability to blend in whatever environment it chooses (to protect itself). The downfall of this characteristic is that it is always becoming what others are (trying to fit in) or who others want it to be; therefore not making a true definition for its own person. Without knowledge of self, relationships with others will not last long or will always breed difficulty. Common said it best, "never find a man 'til you find yourself". I agree.

You can imagine that I attract all types of men with all of those different looks previously mentioned. It just depends on which Rae wants to be on the scene that night or the type of event I'm attending. I'm thinking finding myself will breed consistency in my style or look. When you're lost, you'll try everything (hairstyles and men). Next stop for me, dreads perhaps? We'll see...

Once upon a time I was dating a guy, and he was very reserved and introverted. Y'all know I'm highly extroverted, and was just being myself by changing up my hairstyles to match my outgoing personality. He hated it! So the decision was to wear it like he liked it or just be me. I didn't choose the latter initially. Needless to say the relationship was short-lived. If you can't be yourself, you shouldn't stay in a stifling relationship. In conclusion, he broke it off. Thanks for the favor I say!!

Remember ladies, it's about what's within that truly matters; not hot shoes and Birkins. Men don't care about those until you ask them for money...and don't hesitate to try being "prudish" for a day...He will feel 16 again. Like the man in the movie from Down Under (Australia) said "the forbidden is a huge turn on"...I'm Catholic and sometimes Baptist. We grew up wearing pantyhose and skirts to the knee...men like pantyhose...

Many of us truly desire what we can't have and what appears to be unattainable...sometimes it's unfortunate, but the one who can get the man or woman they want to want them badly enough as well, has truly mastered the law of attraction which often involves a bit of detachment.

"Paradox Man"

Keeps me guessing...
Keeps me hooked...
It's a paradox
Because I know he has other women
But makes me feel I'm the "One"
He's a Paradox Man
Saying all the right things
And hitting all the right notes...
Keeps me mesmerized and hypnotized...
And this he knows
He's not a "Player"
You know what to expect
You know what you're getting yourself into
When dealing with him
He's more like a Pimp
Gives you just enough to keep you
He knows all about you
And how to really get to you
To get what he wants
What he wants is his Freedom
To do as he pleases
He is everything you need
At particular moments...
He's your latest accessory,
He's your friend,

He's your confidant,
He's your lover
He's preparing you to meet him halfway…
To become one with him…
But don't be fooled
He's dangerous as they come
Your heart will be won…
Even taps into the Spiritual Essence of your Soul
When you need a lift
Fine like wine
And sunshine to your rainy day…
But he's a paradox
Because he's not just for you…
His heart belongs to HER too…

r. Big, Mr. Big, I call him Mr. Big. Mr. Big, Mr. Big for so many apparent reasons. So who is Mr. Big? Now you know I'm not going to name any names, but I will tell you what a Mr. Big is. For starters, Mr. Big is generally 5 to 15 years your senior. Okay, we got that out the way. Next, there are many apparent reasons why he's Mr. Big and not always because of his size. Mr. Big, yes he's older; he's established; he has met every criteria on your wish list. He is someone you can look up to; he has just about everything you have or are working to build for your life so why not admire or aspire to be in the company of such a "Big" man, as in "Bigtime". He's also usually pretty well-known in your community because of an established occupation (perhaps something entrepreneurial), philanthropic efforts, or maybe he's just a "Big" socialite in your city or town.

This type of man attracts women of all ages and genres whether he is single or not. The Mr. Big I'm speaking of happens to be a single one. Generally, Bigs have been previously married and may possess children almost your age or at least half your age. He doesn't come with much drama unless he's a messy Mr. Big, but remember his reputation in the community is on the line so he has to remain as drama-less as possible.

How I met Mr. Big? I know you are wondering...Yes Love Doctor how? Well, I was 24 years young...hot and fresh to death...you feel me...I was so fine that I didn't know I was fine...slim and trim...carefree, footloose and fancy free...you feel me? Mr. Bigs are definitely attracted to this type...A young, educated, fly, fit, young woman...working toward big dreams (Masters degree attainment at the time). I was just living it up! Living life to the fullest! I was so enjoying my life at the time that I didn't pay Mr. Big any mind. I think he was on his way up then...but heck all I knew was you are 10yrs older than me...older than my sibling, and I wasn't sure how to react. Had I known then what I know now...I would have tried to lock him down then. Ya know?

You have to catch these types when you first meet them when they are into you and in pursuit because if you don't, later on down the line when you try to get at him on a serious note...like "hey what's up Mr. Big I'm ready to get married and have kids now"...he will start smelling himself and forget how he pursued you...he will develop what I've coined as the "Mike Jones Syndrome". And that's not a pretty sight because he will officially play with you because he knows that now you're ready. See it was better for him when you weren't ready because that gave him more time to enjoy being in an uncommitted, "touch and go" relationship with you and whomever else. As you begin to age, he will still look at you like you are 21 or 24, that first day he met you and was so captivated by your beauty. However, it will never be the same if you did not accept his initial advances.

Do you get where I'm going with this one? Mr. Big is your ideal partner, if you don't mind the age difference, but his ego is so enormous that it will take some time to get him down the aisle, if he's never been married, and back down the aisle if he has. And don't think you are going to come at him trying to produce any children out of wedlock...again, the rep is on the line...unless you actually catch him slipping one night which would be a rare occasion. This man is good to keep around because he knows many people whom you may need contact with so try to maintain a healthy relationship with this one.

In conclusion, if you are not ready for the Big Leagues, Mr. Big is not for you. If you don't mind a rollercoaster ride then it may be fun, just realize what you are getting yourself into…with Mr. Big comes increased responsibility to stay on point in all of your personal endeavors. Since you are no longer 21, he's not going for the "damsel in distress" routine either. Sometimes the rules with him are clean cut, and sometimes there are no rules. The real truth, he's not ready to settle down because if he was, then he would. If you are the chosen one woman for him…you will know it. There are no excuses left to come from a man who has everything…if he's not willing to share with you, then you're just not the one. And throughout the years, you will not be able to change the dynamic of the relationship. "The Thrill Is Gone"…Be his toy or keep it moving, because another fine, young, tender thing is waiting in the wings to catch a ride with Mr. Big… but remember he's aging too!

Part IV
Self-Love: Walk the Talk

Pretty Girls Pt. 2
"Paradox Woman"

I AM the Paradox Woman
I'm not a "what you see is what you get"
I'm pretty...
In fact beautiful

Don't blame me
I'm just evolving
Like a caterpillar
Into a butterfly
On a cold lonely night

But all is not lost
I am found
By Me
So His admiration
Means nothing to me

I admire me
And who I'm becoming
Still pretty
Still strong
Still a paradox

It's not for you to figure me out
I figure me out
I shape and mold me
Into what I see

I define me by my inner beauty
That you may not see initially
See I'm the paradox
You don't even know what I require of thee
But you must govern yourself accordingly…
The Gentleman mind knows exactly what I mean

The Joys of Being Single

I have been single for so long now that I am really starting to appreciate it; and here's why:

1. You don't have to cook if you don't want to.
2. You don't have to clean up after anyone or yourself for that matter.
3. You don't have to pretend to like ESPN or any other male-dominated channel.
4. You don't have to keep beer in the refrigerator.
5. The toilet seat is always down.
6. You don't have to call and "check-in" with anyone.
7. You don't have to share your side of the bed or your pillows.
8. You can stay on the phone with your girls or your Mom all night without anyone looking at you sideways.
9. You can take trips with your girlfriends and not have to wonder "what he's doing".
10. You don't have to worry about anyone cheating on you.
11. You don't have to comb your hair or look cute or put on makeup if you don't feel like it (or shower) T.M.I. huh? (I'm going green that's all just conserving the water).
12. You just have so much liberty without having to explain yourself to anyone.

13. You can sleep naked without worrying about someone randomly touching you.
14. You can flirt with or dance with as many guys as you wish when you're at a party.
15. You can go on as many dates as you like with whomever you like and not have to pay.
16. It's really all about you!!

It's not that I don't still have the desire for a mate, it's just that I've been re-focusing my energy on me and what I truly want out of life. Being in a relationship with another person is no longer my TOP priority. My relationship with myself is becoming the most important one. If I don't love me, or even like living with me, a mate will not make the situation better, only worse. Seeing myself and my flaws and working on these things has been so rewarding for me at this time. I am loving everything about me; even the things that I don't like about me. We must all know ourselves; love ourselves; and learn to live with ourselves before we can truly add to someone else's life. In a recent book I'm reading (Look Before You Love: Feng Shui Techniques that Reveal Anyone's True Nature by Nancilee Wydra) the author states, "the journey will begin only when you are ready". If we are truly ready, we have to make room and do the work. We want to be a balanced person and attract a balanced mate as well.

The truth is the only place you can "look" for love is within. You must first come face to face with all of your own issues before you are recognizable or "divinely" attractive to your mate; and before you will actually even recognize this special person. Look in the mirror…you might actually see yourself "flaws and all"…and your mate will too. This person will be just as ready for you as you are ready for you; and them!

There are many books out there on this same topic that mention some of my same reasons. Let's make being single fun again!

"Suga Mama"

"Suga Mama"
That's what they call me...
Or is it "Miss Raechel"?
I forget my age on nights like this...
But all we did was dance and kiss

Brown Suga Mama
That's what they call me...
Because I'm sweet with my smooth Brown-Skin
Drivin' those young men wild
Or is it the other way around?

Nights like this I forget my age...
And my race
Most black women wouldn't live to tell you about this

Suga Mama that's what they call me...
Nights like this I forget my age
But age is just a number
And love is blind to color
Or is it lust?

Nights like this I forget my age...
I guess that's why they call me
"Suga Mama"

Interracial Dating, Cougar Life, and the Sexual Energy of 22 Year Old Men

*L*ong title for an entry I know…It could probably be a book within itself. Initially, this was supposed to only be about interracial dating, but I had such an exhilarating weekend that I needed to include all topics. So here goes.

As the weekend comes to a close and I contain the spirit of Sexual Goddess "Blanche Devereaux", you remember our Golden Girl, Rue McClanahan, as well as other sexy Cougars; Samantha from Sex and the City; Mariah Carey; Demi Moore; and "Ms. Berry Ms. Berry", who we all know as Halle; I have to reflect upon my own Goddess energy which has recently created an influx of young male attraction. Lawd, I must be glowing or something!! Pure Self-Love in full effect and taking flight…the almost 30 vibe and loving it!!

As you know since May 1st I've shed at least 15 to 20lbs, which was the goal for my 30th Birthday on September 25th. Well weight loss brings with it an exuberant flow of confidence, which we all know is very attractive and sexy. I just didn't know that dropping 20 would draw in sooooo many men. Whew! I'm overwhelmed! Oh and not just any men; 22 year old men! Mercy! I feel like "fresh meat" all over again only with some wisdom this time. I mean they are black (African-American); they are white (of European descent); heck they are even of mixed race descent (like I don't know the ethnic background), which I believe we all have something in us if we were born and raised in the heart of what we now know as America.

All I know is that I'm feeling like "Rae the Cougar", more so in theory not practice; for all you scholars. And for the non-scholars, it just means that the "Youngins" have caused me to really consider this whole Cougar thing, but I haven't actually begun practicing the ideal. (just keeping it PC... politically correct) Let's just say that flirting with the idea has really been fun and entertaining. I honestly feel 22 again. (smile). One of my young white boys told me I was "vibrant". (He actually has a very strong energy...whew I can still feel that...lol). I think they even forget that I'll be 30 next month. Ha ha! It's cool though. These young 20 something males have such a powerful energy. They just draw me in...lol... there is something to be said again about Soul connections. You can feel how they supersede the physical realm. The Soul is who we are outside of this body. We all look very different outside of this body than in this body. I'm sure we all look identical outside of this body...possibly. What does Spirit look like? Just think about that for a moment. The most racist person is obviously out of touch with what is and has happened on a Soul level. Hmm...makes you think...

We are all approaching a new level of consciousness as the world continually evolves...so it's not a surprise that I can connect with the consciousness and energy of the 22 year old male (despite race), if he is an open-minded and free Spirit such as myself. I'm thinking that Spirit knows no age...I do know that love is blind so in turn love is ageless (so no more trying to figure out Ashton and Demi or Nick and Mariah). I'm learning that any situations that I've previously misjudged, I'm being confronted with; and I'm totally okay with the learning process. It feels good. And I just love new experiences and sharing them.

For so long, some Sistahs have been giving some Brothas

such a difficult time about their choice to date outside of their race. I used to be one of those women. Angry, single, black woman; well not anymore. Some of my best friends and favorite people would not be alive if it were not for interracial dating, mating, and relating. As I began to release that hatred, I also began attracting my own interracial dating experiences. Sure there are a few cultural differences, but there is also so much to learn and share with each other. Now we all may have a preference for who we would like to marry and bring home to mom and dad. The truth here is that, whomever you prefer to bring home, is who you will bring home. That's really all I have to say about that one. I have a long list of the characteristics of who I would like to bring home...all the way down to even a preference in race. However, I happen to enjoy the company of men and meeting even culturally different ones. I have not stepped foot outside of this country yet, but have been afforded the opportunity to meet and mingle with such diverse people. I feel blessed to have encountered these experiences; that some people may never have because of fear or any other personal barriers they may possess.

Soulmate

If I never see you again,
I can say that I loved you.
I can say that I felt like
You were my Soulmate.

Maybe the timing just wasn't right
Or maybe we just couldn't get it right,
But I can say that I loved you.

I don't quite understand why I do,
But I love you for you.
I can say that I loved you…

I love you…
Your smile, your walk, your way
Your laugh…
You make me smile—

I want to be with you,
See you,
Hold you…
I can say that I loved you…

Soulmates: The Epilogue

"Journey to Self: Journey to Love" is my comprehensive "dissertation" on love in life. It is through self-critique, self-evaluation, and self-realization that one can make a journey through what can sometimes appear to be a complex love life. Knowledge of self and self-love are the keys to a healthy life and healthy relationships. The most important relationship that we can ever have is the one with Self. When we are balanced within, we can attract a balanced mate. People will always mirror to us what we don't always notice about ourselves; the good, the bad, and the ugly.

When my Mentor first told me this, it went way over my head. It all makes sense to me now; especially when you begin to follow a Divine Path and start listening to your Higher Self (the God within). You honestly don't have to look for love… it is within…that which you feel you lack will be lacking (missing)…if you know that you are love and come from love…you will always have love and won't have to look. (That was inspired by Dr. Wayne Dyer). You must be satisfied with self, but also have a teachable Spirit and be willing to learn from others. What I've learned is that "religiosity" is going to keep people from True Love (God). There are some "rules" that can be followed for disciplinary matters; however true love is guilt free and able to walk in the Abundance of Love, which is God. "God is Love".

I believe that I have several Soulmates out there. Now

here's a concept that most cannot fathom. My Mentor's Husband suggested this to me at one time; again, it went way over my head. The truth is, on a subconscious level, we choose our Soulmates and experiences. These experiences have already occurred in another realm; so good or bad, we have somehow attracted various experiences into our life as we know it. Our Soulmates can also be derived from our past lives, which may include some unfinished business with these individuals. Next time you meet someone, simply ask in your head or out loud, "What did you come to teach me?" "What do I need to learn about myself from my encounter with you?" We are free to decide how to handle these experiences and how to move forward into a life filled with love, peace, and joy, which is our true Godly, Godlike nature. The opposite end of the spectrum is our dark nature. At any given time, we have the ability and power to choose which nature we want to exist within us. I favor the lighter, happier side of life, but at times, the dark side will creep in and this is the result of not being in balance. We have to balance the spectrum in order to live the good life that we desire.

Soulmate 1: My supposed "Twin Flame" (The Beginning)- He helped me start this book "Journey to Self: Journey to Love". He is difficult to tack down. He's a gift to the world, like a "Star" or a light for all. He's almost "just like me". We even look alike. He intuitively knows me (scary)... even finishes my sentences. He's psychic and loves children (Libra)...aw...especially his own.

Soulmate 2: The "Husband" Material (Cancer) (The Middle)- He looks excellent on paper and is sharp as a tack! He's fine and cleans up well! He's aging gracefully. This is the one to bring home to Mama. We call him "Mr. Big" because he has it all; except me. He's been around for a few years, but caught me off guard while on this journey. He's also a "light" who is kind of difficult to pin down. Actually, he's a little secretive like me; his inner circle is very tight; yet he's a Social Butterfly; same as me.

Soulmate 3: The "Superstar" (The Tail)- He is a world traveler (Sagittarius). He gets around. He has that "Diddy Swag" and is a true Entrepreneur. You can't put him in one category though…he's just a "Hustler". He is ambitious and unforgettable. He truly desires to settle down; but not until he sees and touches the world (which he's already doing) with those "Amber" colored eyes. He's the $5 million dollar man who aspires to move to an island or somewhere secluded to enjoy his money and all his accomplishments. I may have to join him.

Dr. Wayne Dyer says that a Soulmate is a person who "teaches you the most"…and "that you can't get rid of them". They can be family members or Sister-friends and play-brothers. Again, I have several Soulmates. So who will be the lucky winner? Who will steal Dr. Rae's heart and put some "bling" on the finger? I and the world await the answer. He may be none of these three. All I know is I plan to be happy with or without a man.

I AM Love…I'm filled with Love…it overtakes me and surrounds me…I give love abundantly as it is given unto me…I choose love. One way to choose is to learn to live without that which you desire. Detach and it will overtake you…

You were in my dream last night…
In my subconscious…
In my future…my past…
My present…I see

Wanting,
Longing for the Manifestation of Desires
Will and Emotion

This love potion
You allowed me to drink of you…
Be with you in my mind…

Feel you to the depths that bind…
Unwind, rewind, take a walk with me…
See me for me

Here waiting
And Ready to love you…

Heart, body, and soul…
No need to control
Impulse Divine
'Cause you are mine
And I'm yours,
Forever and Ever,
Amen…

Twin Flames:
Meet Katherine and Brody (True Love)

August 18, 2010

Iwas blessed to be in the presence of such a beautiful young (twenty-something) couple today; Kathryn and Brody. We were only working together a few days before I began to notice how similar they are. So today I said to Kathryn, "you guys remind me of each other". I mean even from the way they talk and even how they look (in appearance). They are also two of the most beautiful people individually and when they are together. They appear to be two evolved souls when they are together and apart. Interestingly enough, they are both English majors in school; go figure. They are also prone to attracting homeless animals together, with the consideration of "healing" or "taking in" these friends from God. They have been dating for about two years and are happily engaged. Their presence together is so powerful that I even felt myself "blushing" just to think of the love they share with each other. There is really something spiritual about being with your "other half". Now this is not to say that they are perfect as Kathryn stated, "we are not perfect". They get on each other's nerves sometimes; which happens in every type of relationship. No two spirits are alike, but they come together to complement each other. They are "one" and come from the same Source, but one is male energy and the other female energy. I was elated to witness such young love that was pure in heart and Spirit.

Being around this couple made me reflect on my Twin Flame. Is a Twin Flame, Soulmate, other half found in each Lifetime? Just because you find this person, does this mean that you get to ultimately be with this person? Or do you wait until next lifetime like Erykah Badu? Lots of questions here huh? The two Souls must evolve individually, and sometimes work through some major barriers before finding one another and finding their way back to their Creator. There is a huge purpose for the meeting of two evolved Souls. A life purpose; there is work to be done in the Earth. So in fact, it may take several lifetimes before they actually figure out this "thing called life". This is why the "Journey to Self: Journey to Love" is so relevant to life. There is a reason to live. Not just to have fun and enjoy the pleasures of life; which is also a nice benefit to living, but to really work. Why was I created? This is a major question of life...

A Twin Flame, a Soulmate is here to assist you in answering those questions...they are here to help you figure it out as they figure it out...and they assist you back to your original Spirit state...and to God. God is the "One"...and You, male or female energy, plus your Soulmate's male or female energy is equal to the One. This is why we are in search of the One who is God (within and without...as it is within so it is without). In this life and Earthly realm at times we get it confused. Your Soulmate is not God...you are not God, but together you exemplify the energy that makes up God, the One, the male and female energy that is God.

God works! And we are here to work! We play, we learn, we evolve, we work! Sound easy? Sound fun? Well, it's not always easy, but it doesn't have to be as difficult as we make it. The objective here...if you come into contact with this person, don't take it lightly. People have always told me "you will know". Hmm...each day, especially since my encounter with him (the male version of me)...I surely believe that... you will know. You can look this person in the eyes and see yourself. They will mirror you back to you. They will teach you...they will learn from you...they will grow with you. Until the work is complete...in this lifetime or the next...

Think of the couples who inspire you...it could be your parents or your grandparents approaching fifty years or so of marriage. Can you see yourself growing together with someone in that capacity? At the age of 20 or 30, who really knows who the One is? It could be someone from your childhood...we've all heard the stories..."after college he or she found me" or even check out the movie called the "Time Traveler's Wife"...the man traveled from one century to the next but continued to make his way back to a little girl... who grew up to be his wife...Is your mind blown yet? Ha ha...mine is. The truth...we don't know what's going on in other realms unless we investigate them. Do we really want to know? Are we afraid of the truth? What about the man who visits me in my dreams (him)? Is this the other realm (lifetime) taking place? Makes you go hmm...

The lasting relationships of those we admire took time to grow into that life-long loving commitment; I imagine met with some growing pains depending on what happened before they came together. Despite any barriers, the outcome is beautiful. A life of love; working together or raising a family together; whatever their purpose has become. When it's all said and done, they chose love. I choose love today! Love of God, love of Self, and love of Others!

"Love Is..."

A Haiku for Dana

Love is why I live...
Love is who I am in Life...
Life is why I love...

"Brown Sugar"

Your lips are like Brown Sugar to me...
The lingering of your sweet honey
Dew drops that melt in my mouth
Your kiss is like Brown Sugar to me...
I want some of your Brown Sugar...

"Brown Sugar"
Now What's That?

What is it about brown sugar that catches your sweet tooth? It's a certain kind of sweet; not sweet like white sugar though. From the taste, to the color, to the consistency, it's just something about this type of sugar that when added to a bowl of flour, butter, eggs, and oil it just gives the dessert you're making the right touch. Not too sweet but just enough to make it taste just right! What is it about "brown sugar" that can make a man or a woman lose his or her mind? First of all, what is brown sugar? Well, it must be so good that D'Angelo had to sing a song about it; and hey Taye Diggs starred in a movie called "Brown Sugar". So what is this thing, and how can I get my hands on it?

For me Brown Sugar is...that sweet feeling when you first meet someone...that first point of contact...it's never too sweet...it's always just right. It adds flavor to your life without overpowering you...it is simple...and uncomplicated. Drama-free...it's a spice of life. It's the point in a relationship that just is and exists. It's not the main ingredient of the relationship, but its extra flavoring makes things sweet...nice...calm and pleasant.

So I posed the question to my peers, what is Brown Sugar to you and here's what they said:

"What is brown sugar?? It's unique, attractive, yet sweet with every taste". --Jeradiah

"A delightful sugar used for baking chocolate chip cookies?" --Kate

"It's great for BBQ sauces & baked beans... it comes in dark brown & light brown". --LaKristal

"As in 'Brown Sugar' the film..it was defined as the sweetness of black life and best of black friendship". –Michael

"Anything sweet". --Erin

"A woman who is equally sexy in a business suit and cocktail dress". --Sunnie

As you can see, no one had anything negative to say about their experiences with brown sugar. So see whether you are cooking up a treat or a meal or out on the town mingling, brown sugar will always be that little sumthin' sumthin' that adds flavor.

Have you found the Brown Sugar in your life? Do you represent this sweet spice of life? You attract that which you are. Can you learn to be sweet but not too overbearing in your love relationships? Can you accept someone adding a sweet flavoring to your life, and can you be that flavoring? I know one thing, I'm looking for my "Brown Sugar"; I've got a major sweet tooth. In the meantime, I'm working on just being that brown sugar. It's not a difficult task…

Lovin' Me

I'm feelin' myself...
Like never before...
This isn't arrogance
Or false confidence
It's Love...
Real Love...

I've waited my whole life for this moment
A Rebirth
I'm lovin' everything about me too
Every curve, every blemish
And every kink

So cheers to all the jerks who didn't want me
And thanks to the fools who let me go
I love me and that's all that matters
30 is not the new 20,
Baby it's better!!

Wave Goodbye to these 20s
Say Hello to the 30s
The "New Rules" for 30 & Beyond:
What the 20s Taught Us in Love & Relationships

1. Do not be a "Stalker"…online (FB) or off line for that
    matter. You will always find out something you don't
    want to see or know, and there are plenty of constructive
    things that you can be doing with your time. Read a book
    or do something to further develop yourself.

2. Do not knowingly be a "Side-Chick"…unless it's just
    that good and discretion is your best friend. Being
    someone's side dish instead of his main course is never
    cute, especially not at 30 and beyond…you are just too
    grown for that. There is not a shortage of men. Enjoy
    your "you" time or family time.

3. Always protect yourself and/or use some type of birth
    control… if you are not ready for children or if you are
    unmarried. An unplanned pregnancy or an unexpected
    visit to the doctor can be detrimental for you and your
    partner. Just wrap it up! Or enjoy yourself instead.
    Nothing wrong with celibacy when you're single and out
    of your 20s…it's safer that way and uncomplicated.

4. Take care of your health. Eat right. Exercise. Yoga or

something. At 30 and beyond, your health should be top priority. You have to be healthy to raise children and watch them grow as well as to do everything in life even to work. You will be much happier about life after shedding a few pounds. If you don't have time…make the time. When your body is healthy, you are healthy…mentally, physically, and emotionally. It's not an overnight thing… but be cognizant of what's going in…and hope that it's coming out as well.

5. Never ever ever…chase a man! It never has been and never will be cute…ever in life. Promise yourself that you will never do it again in this Lifetime or the next. Expressing interest and flirting is one thing…but hunting him down…serial texting him, blowing up his phone, etc…will help you lose every time. If he was interested, he just lost interest after that 3rd text and fourth email you sent him. And didn't give him a chance to respond. (This may go both ways for the fellas too; you will know when a woman is truly interested in you). Men at any age can smell desperation like a dog smells fear…he will either take advantage of you or ignore you.

6. Go on way more dates…than booty calls. If you have more booty calls than dates, you should definitely re-evaluate your life plan. You did not just discover sex…nothing is open after Midnight, except 7/11 and Walmart. Sex can always wait. Try to really get to know the man before hopping into the sack. You will respect yourself in the morning. Just because he bought you dinner, it doesn't mean you have to give him dessert at your place. Just chill out.

7. No more Community Service Project dating. If he's

broke, let him remain. If he's not that attractive to you, don't try to fix him up. If he has low self-esteem, run. If he's under-educated, don't convince him that school is the way unless he asks you about it. Just give it up. Don't put more time into helping someone else than you do for yourself...just work on you until Mr. Right shows up. Mr. Right may not have everything you want when you meet him, but don't allow anyone to use you up.

8. Trust your Intuition. If you think he's lying, 9 times out of 10, he is. If you think he has a girlfriend, he probably does. If you think he's a player, yep, you've guessed it... Sometimes we can be wrong about our initial assessment of a man. If he seems too good to be true...let that be the guiding light. Trust your gut feelings and pray and consult friends and family who can be honest with you; those who are not jaded. Definitely get an objective perspective in your dealings with someone who seems a little shady, secretive, or dishonest. Don't be fooled by love or (infatuation).

9. To the best of your ability, be honest with yourself and others. Know what you want from a man. Most of the time, when we meet someone, we know exactly what we want after the first conversation, date, or text/email contact. Try not to mislead yourself or others. You will know if the chemistry is only suggesting for you to be friends or something more. Slow is good. Let the relationship unfold as it may...and try not to rush into something. He knows that you are 30 and beyond and ready to settle down and that he is too...unless he's a Youngin'... If you don't have children, or if you want more children, try to discuss this early on...make sure

you are on the same page. Let the man put a ring on it before you decide to play house!

10. Just be easy. Find out what the 30s have in store for you. Aspire to have the good life that you desire and see it through. Praise God that you made it out of the 20s!

Part V
Rebirth: The Journey Continues

"Rain"

Wash Me
Cleanse Me
Purify Me

I am Renewed, Refreshed, Rejuvenated
Your Power Impacts Me

Fills Me
Heals Me
I Welcome You
Rain On Me!

A Sprinkle, A Mist, A Storm
I welcome you,
I hear you on my window
And at my door

I welcome you
And all you represent:

Abundance
Life
Growth
Maturity
Strength
Change

I welcome you

I accept your Purpose
And Will for my life

Rain on me...

Rae's Guide to Loving Her "Future" Man

First let me start off by saying that I've had the privilege to observe a great deal from my parents and their marriage/relationship…the good, the bad, and the ugly. In the end, they have stayed together for many…many years… and many, many changes. I have been able to watch a woman (mom) and a man (dad) love…no matter the circumstances… even in the unlovable times…and that is a great example… and an example of how God love's us. Unconditionally.

We can learn a lot from these "old school" players…if Dad was a player, Mom had to be one too, because how else did she land him? I'm just saying!

So here's to hoping that I'm not single for too much longer…

So here goes:
1. Don't tear him down, build him up!
2. Pray for him.
3. Listen to him.
4. Have patience.
5. Do not be self-seeking.
6. Be self-less.
7. He doesn't need two Mamas.
8. Be strong, but allow him to be a man (stronger).
9. Respect him.
10. Love him unconditionally and God will do the rest.
11. Know when to speak (your mind) and when not to.

12. Don't use the bedroom or sex (withholding or not) to get what you want.
13. Talk TO him, not AT him.
14. Pray with him.
15. Don't curse (cuss) at him.
16. Bless him.
17. Encourage him.
18. Don't tell all of your business to your friends.

This is my thing…if you are in a relationship, are you happy? Are you with the person that you really want to be with? We have all heard and read all of these advice books… but I've decided to take my own. You have to trust God in this process. This list is somewhat extensive, but I say it's worth a try. But you can't just use this list for any 'ole body. You have to know that you and your guy or potential guy are on the same page. Is he using you? Playing with you like a toy? Then he is not the one to be praying for…yeah, praying that he disappears from your life! For real!

How can you tell the "real" from the "fake" though? I think it has a lot to do with when you first meet a person. Your spirit will tell you what the deal is…if you are still confused, then really pray about it…God will show you…and the truth will always be revealed about that person.

Additionally, your "Man" should be exercising these same practices on you. This list works both ways fellas. I've had guys who wanted to act like a "Daddy". I was thinking, I have two Dads, one is deceased and the other is in St. Louis, MO…thank you very much! And a Granddaddy…so I don't need someone trying to run this. So think of how he might feel when we try to run him, or tell him what to do, or what he needs or should be doing. Sometimes, we need to let them figure it out on their own.

And let them figure out that this woman is the truth! If he can't handle a real and praying woman, then drop him! If he is someone else's Husband or Man, you don't want that either! I'm just saying. Pray that God sends your Man...not Judy's...and ask God to reveal the truth about the man you desire...and He will.

Lastly but not leastly, keep the faith!! If your man or potential man is working on something...let him do that... and don't be offended when what he's working on is not your relationship or potential relationship...It's hard for me as a woman (I want the Husband...the money, the career, the kids, the dog, the 5 bedroom house with the white fence, and the Mercedes...yesterday!!) okay...all of that...that takes time to build up...so let that man work now so that you can live like that by 40.

We live in a Microwave generation...you know we want that "quick fix"...now by the time we reach 30...we have some undoing to do regarding baggage...and this takes time for God to fix...to get you ready for your Husband and him ready for you...

My Greatest Love

How many was does He say that He loves me?
An Infinite amount
And I'm not talking about a man
He always listens to me,
He knows what I'm going to say before I say it,
Knows what I'm thinking...
Knows and gives me what I need before I even ask

He's also very intimate, and patient, and kind toward me...
He always protects me from harm
He watches me while I sleep...
He greets me every morning with
sweet songs from birds singing
And a beautiful sun shining...

He is my greatest love...
He knows me best...
How will I ever repay Him or love Him
As much as He loves me?
He is Self-less and asks for nothing in return...
He is my greatest love of all...

Divine Timing: God's Timing

*L*ast night I met with a new Sister Circle; it was a divinely created opportunity to fellowship with an old friend and one new friend. During our meeting, we exchanged information about the current states of our love lives, and did our best to give each other objective feedback. There was a constant theme that emerged as we discussed the special men in our lives. That theme was "timing". God's timing. Timing is everything in life. Sometimes you can be late for events, on time, or early. Well in each of our situations, we realized that we were a little early. As believers in the Most High God, who knows exactly what we need and when, we decided to surrender all and everything regarding these situations.

I'm thinking what a great way to end my book. My journey is far from over; it is in fact just getting started. The Journey to Self: Journey to Love is not a one time event. Yes, it is a series of events that I've displayed here, but all those things that happened in the love relationships of my twenties were just preparing me for what's ahead. Now, the real work begins. The test is whether or not I practice what I preach. I will definitely be using my own book as a resource for the journey. I have a special love in my life, but actually the relationship is only a seed because its current state is not exactly where I want it to be. I've learned through it all the art of surrendering and detachment. Detachment is not necessarily a bad thing. It's actually safe. It means that

I choose to take care of my own heart and my own needs before I try to give my all to a physical man; who is only flesh like me. Yes, he has a spirit, but his spirit can never replace the spirit of God.

Often as humans, we become addicted to the tangible; what we can feel, see, hear, and touch. We have to learn to feel, see, hear, and touch God as well. God is always there waiting for us to search Him out. To become so filled with His love that no situation can tear us down, and you know that we (women) are some emotional creatures! No matter what our love life looks like; no matter what our finances look like; no matter who has hurt us in the past; we learn to operate in love at all times! Love of Self, Love of Creator, and then we are better able to love others the way God intended.

I am excited about the future! God's Word says, "I know well the plans I have for you, plans to prosper you and not harm you, plans to give you hope and a future". I have decided to trust God in every aspect of my life. So when "Boo" is not acting right, who do I turn to? You know who it is! God the Creator is just like a Mom or a Dad; saying, "hey, I'm the one who birthed you out, how dare you not spend any time with me, or question my timing, or what I'm doing in your life"! God knows what's best. He's always working things out for our Highest Good. It is in our surrendering everything to Him, even our own desires, will He then step in and give us a life filled with so many blessings of which we've never even dreamed. I don't know about you, but I'm trusting God with my life and my love life. Always, always trust God first, keep God first, and not man! God is the only Source that can fill the void in your heart so fill up on God before you try to love on anyone else! God will protect your heart if you stay in the palm of His hand...

Love Letter

Like Angel Wings suspended across the
Sky is your Love Letter to me...
No One can love me like you do...
You are the Source of All
I'm filled with You...
You Permeate my Soul...
My Entire Being...
Without You I'm nothing...

$Love$

I am in love with love...
Who is love?
What is love?
God is love.

Do you know God?
Have you tried Him today?
Did you know that He can take <u>ALL</u> your pain away?
He can make a crooked path straight,
And the sun shine even in the rain.

If you haven't tried Him yet
You're surely missing out
But don't believe me
You can take another route!

See I tried that other road
And all I did was fail
But when I sold out for Him
I did nothing but prevail!

Without Him,
I'm nothing
I'm blind and cannot see
The good things within
And on earth, my destiny!

My purpose in life
Becomes clearer everyday,
I'm no longer lost
And suffering comes not my way.

So do me a favor
And don't even look at me,
But take this as a message
From the One who lives in me.

You can call me crazy,
But who am I without Him?
I don't belong to me or to you
And certainly not to them.

But I'm _ALL_ His
And lovin' the way He loves me
He forgives me and lifts me
Gives me security.

So when man fails me
I no longer cry
I look to my Lord
He is my full supply.

So do what you want
And do what you will
But I'll just keep on Praisin'
For I know,
GOD IS REAL!

Extras!

How to Be Happy Exactly Where You Are in Life!

Each day is a new day! Learn from the mistakes or mishaps of yesterday. This is the way to keep moving forward in life and to cultivate a happy life; an inner contentment no matter where you are (geographically); regardless of your income level; or even marital status. Learn to be happy exactly where you are in life; and whatever you don't like about your life or circumstances learn the best ways to go about changing them. Take baby steps because some things do not change overnight. The best and most lasting changes take time and so much effort. Cultivate effort, change, and happiness each day. Do not beat yourself up about yesterday; or even failed relationships or even failed job situations. Move forward into tomorrow with a positive outlook and work to get the best out of each day. And some days, just take it easy and relax. You can be happy exactly where you are in life today!

Happiness really has to come from within. What makes you happy in life? You have to decide this for yourself. Can you still be happy on your worst day or when things don't go your way? Sometimes, you just have a good day and other times you have bad days, but you have to choose happiness. Today was a good day for me. Why? Well, some things went my way. At times, things come along that feel like struggle, but when those things begin to resolve you can do nothing but be happy and filled with joy! We would like everyday to be like this, but the truth is sometimes life will test your endurance and ability to cultivate your happiness. For some people having a love life makes them happy, for others it is their children, and for others maybe it is their occupation. Maybe for some it is a combination of it all. Can a person truly have it all? I believe so, but I also believe that this takes some work. We have to decide what makes us happy, and what are we living for or doing in life to cultivate that euphoric state of happiness!

Light Skin
Dark Skin
Black and White
That's what I see today
When I observe this fight.

This struggle
For Money, Power, and Success
The lack of harmony
Brings nothing but Stress.

The Yin and the Yang
Over there holding hands
Understand the true meaning
Of the Law of the Lands.

It's love. Although
It may not be true,
But Opposites Attract
Don't let the fools fool you.

I like his blue eyes;
His blond hair to match.
You like his bronze tan;
That black curly-haired catch.

Love sees no color
No ethnicity
Love has its own culture
That's how things should be.

There's no way in love that shame should exist.
There's no way in love that poverty should persist.
They don't know love.
Money makes them blind,
And Power is Control,
And Success is Divine.

There is no room
For the innocent slacker.
Born into confusion
Attracted to the illusion.

The comfort, the necessities
And waste money brings,
Lured and enticed
By sex, cars, and bling blings.

But it's all human nature
We enjoy pricy treasures
We want to look good
We want to feel pleasures.

When will it all end?
It seems things just get worse.
It's apart of the plan
The love, the hate, the hurts!

When will it all end?
No one seems to know.

It may end tomorrow
Or sooner,
You think so?

The nature of the beast
Is only to be wild
To be tamed
Defamed,
And treated like a child.

A child is so pure
So real, so sure
When his mind is untainted
He discovers the cure.

The cure to love,
To heal a dying world
For he sees no color
There is peace in his world.

His parents are happy
This is what he sees
He feels, he lives
He wants, he needs.

His life is so precious
His experiences form him
Into the Man of his Purpose
Or the Woman of Adornment.
We still don't understand
Some things are just not perfect
Sometimes roles change
Some other forms surface.

This man is too sweet.
This woman is too strong.
They still remain purposeful
It just appears to be wrong.

Who are we to judge
What we don't comprehend
Should these people be damned?
They need love from within,

The circle, the family, the Angels from above
Will we ever get it right?
Can we just learn to love?

"Destiny"

I feel it getting closer
Nearer to the **Time** and **Season** for Success!

I **Live** it
Walk it
And **Breathe** it everyday!

God has **Blessed** me
To **See** me
Through **His Eyes**
And **All** that He has
Predestined for my **Life**!

Now, my **Dreams** are **Real**!
My **Destiny** is beginning to Surface
Because of my **Faith** in Him!

Thank You

Thank you all for taking this journey with me. Can you see my progress? Can you relate to the journey to self and the journey to love? The road has been bumpy and rocky, but not without getting me to my destination. I am still a work in progress. My goal was to reach out to an audience who could relate and receive the healing and the path. Always remember to work on you continuously. When you are healthy, you attract healthy people into your life. When you walk around defeated, you attract people to prey on you. Love and Life are about learning. Learning about yourself and others; Learning what you want from life; And learning to love yourself and others unconditionally; The way God intended. Never be anyone's doormat! Dust yourself off and LOVE yourself and your life to the FULLEST!

The journey was fun. The journey was painful, but I'm glad I made it through. If you haven't made it through, you will! It was a journey of love and infatuation, to the ultimate Self-Love and fully embracing the love of my Creator! God wants us complete and lacking in nothing. We must first be complete and whole individuals in order to add to someone else's life! Embrace your path and journey to self; your journey to love. God is Love!

--Much Love,

Dr. Rae

P.S. - Be on the look out for the "Self-Love Handbook". Coming Soon!

Authors/Writers/People I Admire

*J*ust wanted to list the people who have been very influential and supportive in my life; and/or who are impacting and doing what I want to do:

Richard "Fr. Rick" Potts
Dr. Maurice "Fr. Mo" Nutt
James Wallace
Fred Smith II
Albert Jackson
Winfred Burns II
Alex Lewis, Ph.D.
Ebrahim Soltani, Ph.D.
Dr. Juanita Bynum II
Michelle McKinney Hammond
Iyanla Vanzant
Maya Angelou
Oprah Winfrey
Tyler Perry
Kendrick "KY" Young
Crystal Perkins-Stell
Monique Greenwood
Djehuty Ma'at Ra
Alexyss K. Tylor
Clinnesha Dillon Sibley
Bishop E. Bernard Jordan

Pastors Charles and Paula Martin
Gia (for her insight)
Lyah Beth LeFlore
Jesk'ka N.L. Washington
Maurice G
Darryl Frierson
Sunnie E. Hughes
Darshaun McAway
Cory "Pharaoh" Robinson
Thomas Easley
Christian Goering, Ph.D.
Steve Hintz
Jeradiah Williams
Craig Thomas
Mary Miller McAteer
Eddie Holman
Rudolph "PJ" Tolar
Doreen Virtue, Ph.D.
Natasha Hoar (fellow Lightworker)
Khaaliq Salim
Asha Peebles

Raechel "Dr. Rae" Rivers was born and raised in St. Louis, MO. She has enjoyed creative writing since childhood, but her love of writing grew even stronger during her college years. "Dr. Rae" prides herself on being able to convey such "real" messages about the journey of love. Her words,  racy at times, are what some readers need to hear; would not otherwise say, and appreciate for truth and honesty about love-life situations. "Journey to Self: Journey to Love" is her first self-published book of many to come. She is the founder and CEO of Free Your Mind Promotions, Productions, and Publications, FYMP3. She has recently completed an Ed.S. in Curriculum and Instruction at the University of Arkansas, Fayetteville; and is a full-time Love Coach specializing in the journey to self-love. Her life's mission involves encouraging women and young women of all ages to "work on you and love yourself just the way you are".

Dr. Rae has written a series of blog entries that she's ready to share with the world beyond her site www.raeluvs2write.blogspot.com as well as her updated site http://drrae.wordpress.com. She was inspired by the support of her followers at www.twitter.com/raeluvs2write as well as readers on www.facebook.com/FaithFulMillionairess . The time is NOW! God has called Dr. Rae to rise to her next level and live out her life's purpose. The objective is to help in healing women and young women from love relationship experiences. The true healing begins by working on Self and knowing that you are enough.

The "Love Doctor" is here to help, and she can be contacted directly at freeyourmindp3@gmail.com for any questions, discussions, or personal topics.